RIDE

DRIVE

LAKE

DRIVE

LAKE

MUSIC PAVILION

HK

TERRACE

REFRESHMENT SALOON

DRIVE

DRIVE

DRIVE

POND

V᛫᛫ AVENUE

The Falconer of Central Park

The Falconer
of
Central Park

Donald Knowler

KARZ-COHL
New York   Princeton
1984

Library of Congress Cataloging in Publication Data

Knowler, Donald, 1946-
The Falconer of Central Park.

1. Bird Watching–New York (State)–Central Park
(N.Y.) 2. Birds–New York (State)–Central Park (N.Y.)
3. Central Park (New York, N.Y.) I. Title.
QL684.N7K6 1984   974.7'1   84-3900
ISBN 0-943828-62-7

Published in the United States by

KARZ-COHL PUBLISHING, INC.

24 Brookstone Drive, Princeton, N.J. 08540

and 320 West 105 Street, New York, N.Y. 10025

Printed in the United States of America

First Edition

For my mother

Over hill, over dale,
Thorough bush, thorough brier,
Over park, over pale,
Thorough flood, thorough fire.

A Midsummer Night's Dream
William Shakespeare

· *Preface* ·

Years ago, experimenting with my camera, I had this idea. I would go into London's Hyde Park, in my native Britain, to photograph a big oak over the course of a year. Twelve photographs taken month by month would chart the seasons and give some tangible shape to their mystery. I never completed the project. There were other trees to see, in more exotic and exciting places.

Years later, I was looking again at an oak—this time in a city now my home, New York. The typewriter had replaced the camera and, in my case, this demanded a greater field of view. I had to look beyond the oak to its immediate environment, Central Park. But the idea of using a calendar year remained the same and during 1982 I got to know not only the oak but all the creatures who depend on it, and the park, for sustenance and sanity.

Donald Knowler
New York
February, 1984

· *January* ·

A kestrel stood guard over the Loch. From his perch in an elm he could see along the untidy streets of Harlem to the north. The reservoir in Central Park lay to the south with the skyscrapers of Fifty-ninth Street and beyond half lost in mist. A gentle rain and low pewter cloud blurred the gauntness of the trees. But the kestrel's vision was on the mark. About two hundred yards away he saw a chickadee working its way up the Loch, prising sleeping bugs from the bark of oaks. The kestrel, the drizzle giving a spiked appearance to its rufous plumage, chose his prey carefully as the chickadee fluttered closer. The kestrel tilted forward on his twig high in the tree, arched his wings and quietly, without a flap, started to swoop. Within seconds the wings were thrown back to act as a brake. The raptor hit the tiny chickadee with a smack. The blow carried the kestrel and the chickadee down into the dip before the kestrel gained control again, with the screaming chickadee in its talons. Slow, powerful flaps were employed now as the kestrel and chickadee rose through a gap in the branches. The other chickadees in the Loch had fallen silent and the bird of prey, out in the clear sky, slowly lowered his head. With precise, hooked beak, he bit into the neck of the chickadee, severing its cervical vertebrae.

•   •   •

It was January 1 in the Loch and a clear stream tumbled over two waterfalls between oak, elm and red maple. Only the rising wail of a police car siren and the rumble of subway trains under Central Park West fixed a time in history. And where once the black bear, the indigenous American and then the European trapper tiptoed in pursuit of deer, the mugger and the wildlife enthusiast tiptoed now.

The presence of the kestrel, and the rain, had washed all signs of life from the Loch. I tramped the stream where blue jays bathe in winter and cottontail rabbits come to drink in spring, climbing above a waterfall near the west section of the park's circular drive. A bedraggled gray squirrel shook rain from its back and scampered over the roots of an oak on the far side of the road.

Someone was following me, but I did not see who.

I headed for the reservoir to the south in the hope of seeing something unusual or unexpected on the sheet of water, some rare species of gull or duck, knowing that at least the familiar wintering ducks would be there. Sure enough, a flotilla of about three hundred lesser scaups was spread out alongside the west wall of the reservoir, with a smattering of canvasbacks and ruddy ducks among them. The three species of duck, traveling thousands of miles to the very center of New York City, had two things in common. They had escaped the biting winter that gripped their breeding grounds to the north and, grouped together, they also felt safety in numbers just in case a predator—like a man with a gun, or the gyrfalcon—should happen by.

I had an uneasy feeling I was not alone. I glanced behind me. No one there. Central Park, the most popular and democratic space in New York City, had become my best friend in the few lonely months I had lived in Manhattan, and I shrugged off warnings of its dangers. It held no menace, but then neither did the streets of the city. I had yet to develop an urban instinct for survival, which New Yorkers call "the smarts," or being "street wise."

As rain spotted the water the ducks were not to know a cold front from the Arctic would reach over them in the coming weeks, freezing the surface of the reservoir and forcing them farther south. The blue, glossy heads of the male scaups were tucked into the fluffy gray feathers of their backs. The canvasbacks also slept, but some of the ruddy ducks chose to dive, scraping algae and other plant life from the bed of the reservoir.

My eyes pressed into binoculars and my body pressed against the wire mesh of the reservoir fence, I did not notice my own predators. I felt something sharp between my shoulder blades, and I turned wildly, like the chickadee when it realized the kestrel was upon it. A man stood with a knife. "Give," he said nervously, a sodden felt hat hiding his face. He was joined by another man, who showed me the central spine of an umbrella, sharp and jagged where it had been snapped in two. I looked about me without moving my head, fearing the slightest movement, the slightest twitch, would signal resistance and get me stabbed. There was no one else in sight, no rescuer, and no point in delaying the surrender of my wallet. So I held it out, and the mugger wearing the felt hat snatched it and ran.

It was pouring with rain now. A storm, which had not stopped a New Year fireworks display in the park, or halted a midnight marathon around the six-mile circular drive, had emptied the park of all but the birds and squirrels by mid-afternoon.

The heavy cumulus clouds lifted on the second day of the year, and the sun drew purple-blue iridescence from the blue jay's plumage. But the temperature was dropping rapidly from the forties of the previous wet twenty-four hours, and ice formed in glassy, uneven layers on wet rocks and footpaths. Despite the cold, the sun produced song from the winter residents of the park. A starling, looking for hibernating grubs, croaked as he turned dead leaves on the Great Lawn. He was chased off by a blue jay. With skeletal trees bare of summer leaves, it was easy to observe the other birds that inhabit the park at this time of the year. A male downy woodpecker darted from bough to bough, finally homing in on an oak and sticking tight to its bark as if drawn there by a magnet. A white-breasted nuthatch walked upside down under a thick limb, probing under the peeling bark with its long beak.

· · ·

Central Park is a backyard for three million New Yorkers, and I was wandering in its 843 acres during those first days in January to pull my thoughts together. I had come to New York in search of something I could not define, to take stock, to find not a new beginning, but an adjustment of course, another avenue. If there had been a constant in my life it had been a casual interest in wildlife and now, for reasons I did not know, I was paying more attention to birds than anything else, drawing irresistible parallels between them and the people using the park.

A New York newspaper reported there was a "straggler" from Europe in the park, and I thought wryly it was a reference to me. I had arrived in New York at short notice, with little preparation, from my native Britain.

The "straggler" was a tufted duck, a very rare bird for North America, and I was keen to see it because I remembered it as a familiar sight in London's parks during my childhood. I was standing against the reservoir fence on the year's second day, a little warier now. The lesser scaups were frozen in the same pose and place as the day before. A male, blinking, raised his head momentarily. A canvasback, his red eye standing out against the rusty color of his head, gave a sleeping female a passing glance as a gust of wind caught him side on and pushed him to the edge of the reservoir. Quickly, he paddled back to join the flock.

The tufted duck did not appear, but I was not particularly concerned that I had missed the species. If the bird had been seen once during the winter there was a good chance it would return, probably from feeding forays farther east or to the Hudson River. On the third day a freezing wind was blowing off the reservoir from the north, and I wrapped a scarf tight around my face as I walked the water's southern rim to the west side where the ducks had been all winter. In front of me, pushing into the reservoir fence so it bulged around him, was a white-haired man, wrapped in concentration. He wore a heavy winter coat, pointed woolen hat, and conical beard—a gnome of a man. He held binoculars to a weathered face, and for a good fifteen minutes he did not move. I cruised by twice, attempting to make conversation, but the bird watcher either did not hear me or was not interested in talking. Finally, and loudly, I uttered the bird watchers' identification call: "Anything about?" The gnome, his white beard showing yellow nicotine stains above the upper lip, mumbled that there was a female ring-necked duck to the north, at the top end of the reservoir a quarter of a mile away. I got the impression he did not want to be disturbed because not once did he lower his binoculars.

"I suppose the report of the tufted duck was just wishful thinking," I said, proceeding to stroll north.

"No, I think I'm looking at a female," said the bird watcher, lowering his binoculars to rest his eyes. I felt a little disappointed that it was only the dull, brown female and not the striking black and white male. The female tufted duck is almost identical to the female scaup, and I could appreciate why the birder did not want to lose sight of it unless he absolutely had to. The duck was sleeping but after a while she raised her head, revealing a slight tuft of brown feathers. "See," said the birder, and in celebration of finding the bird he pulled an unfiltered cigarette from deep inside his coat. He then pointed to the raft of five hundred male and female scaups and declared that a second tufted duck was among them somewhere, and he would find it. I stayed, too—feet frozen, talking of birds.

The birder's name was Lambert and he said he lived in the neighborhood a few blocks from the park. For forty years he had been coming to the park, and he reckoned he had seen more than two hundred species there but had stopped counting. He said that if I had an hour to spare he would show me a book in which the park's regular birders listed the species they had seen. Walking across the Great Lawn, past hooded figures out jogging in the dim light and watching for late afternoon muggers, Lambert told me more about the birds of the park, and the animals, reptiles, and insects. He mentioned the pair of raccoons living under the rotting, disused boats at the Loeb Boathouse. Also the bullfrogs, turtles, and yellow perch in the boating lake, and the strutting killdeers that rest during migration on the Great Lawn. The bird register was contained in a loose-leaf binder chained to the counter of the boathouse cafeteria. The entry recording the tufted duck was in navy blue ink and signed the "Mob" (I later discovered this meant "many old birders"). Someone else claimed to have seen a bald eagle sailing over Broadway in December ("honestly, I did ..."); and squeezed between the duck and eagle entries were details of a mugging. Incidents of robberies and descriptions of muggers were faithfully recorded in navy blue ink along with the birds.

Early in January the population of wintering ducks reached its peak. I counted up to six hundred lesser scaups, twenty of their bigger cousins, greater scaups, forty ruddy ducks and about thirty canvasbacks. With ice creeping over other ponds and lakes in the park, there were more refugees at the reservoir: fifty mallards. These nondiving, dabbling ducks were finding just enough food at the reservoir's edge to sustain them. I quickly learned to pick out the female tufted duck because she would invariably be out of syn-chronization with the flock of scaups. The tufted duck faced north, say, when the scaups were facing south. Even in the center of the flock she was distinct from it: a foreigner, three thousand miles off-course. Sometimes a male scaup would stab out at her with his blunt bill. I was watching the ducks when a husband-and-wife pair of joggers with Christmas present track suits stopped to ask if they could look through my binoculars. "Look at the lovely ducks," panted the hus-band. "Harvey, they're crapping in our drinking water," said his breathless wife.

·   ·   ·

The first snow flurries of the winter, followed by freezing rain, arrived on January 9. Water lapping at the cemented stone sides of the reservoir turned into ice coral as it gripped stems of grass and reeds. The temperature dropped to well below freezing point the following day. Vast tracts of ice formed at the north end of the reservoir and hundreds of ducks had chosen to leave on a journey south to find ice-free wintering areas. Instinct would dictate that a duck move now, while reserves of energy were still strong, in case long flights were necessary.

Most of the United States was undergoing the coldest weather of the century. My hands froze through two pairs of gloves, and somewhere in my heavy boots I had lost my feet. I could not believe New York could get colder than this. But it did the next day—the thermometer at the Central Park weather observatory reading only five degrees Fahren-heit. Mist rose from the rapidly freezing water of the reservoir; air warmed by the sun formed "sea smoke" as it came into contact with the freezing water, the great swirls of moisture meandering in steamy streams. It was beautiful but so cold. Only a handful of lesser and greater scaups hung in now, with three male greater scaups standing out nobly as the sun caught their rounded green heads. The canvasbacks had departed and ten ruddy ducks continued to dive for food in areas of the reservoir which were free of ice. The cold front which had moved in from Russia via the Arctic was dubbed the "Siberian Express" by weathermen and within five days the reservoir had completely frozen over. Giant chunks of ice in different shades of grey formed in strata against the reservoir wall and a low, black cloud forewarned of a six-inch snowfall.

The blizzard arrived during the night, and I was up early to look for raccoon tracks around the boathouse. For an hour I hunted, only to find furrows made by squirrels who were burrowing for food supplies hidden in fall. The squirrels bury more nuts and seeds than they will find and are an important tool in the process of reforestation. The food they do locate is invariably stolen by blue jays, once the cache has been revealed. The jays, not appreciating how deep the snow lay, were submerged momentarily as they pounced on acorns and beechnuts exposed by the squirrels. Emerging, they shook the snow off their beaks with rapid, indignant flicks of the head.

If there is an equivalent in the animal world for a human mugger, I suppose it has to be the blue jay. But the blue jay stops short of outright violence. He is a hustler, a bully but rarely a killer and is usually the first bird to warn others of danger in the woods. The blue jay would be the type of mugger who takes your wallet but leaves you with enough money to take a taxi home, or lets you keep your laundry receipts. A newspaper in the first weeks of January had run a story about a Broadway mugger who gave an out-of-town couple their theater tickets back. He would have been a blue jay mugger.

Abandoning my search for raccoons, I walked past skiers on the circular drive and more blue jays, and headed in the direction of the Ramble, a favorite location for birders. The Ramble forms a thirty-acre sanctuary of woods and glades at the heart of the park and a coating of snow, undulating over low shrubs and smooth rocks, made it a cliché of picture postcard beauty. Virgin snow, with only my footprints in it, I was an ungainly intrusion; slipping and sliding, scarring the white surface, wobbling with arms rigid at my sides like a giant penguin. Around me, the common ground-feeding birds such as the dark-eyed junco, and both the fox and white-throated sparrows barged through the wall of snow, which towered above rotund but small bodies. Smart birds, they gathered under a craggy sourgum, from which bird-feed is suspended during the winter months, and picked up splinters of nuts, lumps of bread and suet, dropped by the birds feeding above them. A plastic soda bottle, with two large holes drilled in the sides, served as a nut dispenser. A blue jay—far too large to squeeze through the holes—flew clumsily into the bottle and tried to grip its smooth sides. The jay, spitting the language of a city taxi driver who does not get a tip, slithered down the container and soon found himself lunging in mid-air, tumbling and crashing into a holly in a spray of powder. The jays were also unsuccessful at two other feeder containers, one a mesh sock holding thistle seed and the other a small wire cage housing suet. The suet swayed tantalizingly, but the jays could not perfect a landing technique, and the cage went spinning on the wire supporting it. The starlings did better, and for once they were not second in line to feed in the winter pecking order.

The starling, smaller than a blue jay, but just as aggressive, is an immigrant to the United States. A batch of sixty birds was released in Central Park in 1890 by a well-meaning gentleman who wanted the birds of William Shake-speare's works around him. The bard's birds have been a problem since. They started breeding immediately and have now spread across virtually the entire country. Like immigrants anywhere, they are earnest and industrious and have created a niche of their own in American avian society at the expense of indigenous species as diverse as the flicker and the Eastern bluebird. In the park it is the flicker that suffers most. The resident starlings seize suitable tree-hole nesting sites before the flickers have arrived from wintering areas in the South. Starlings that have failed to find sites wait for the flickers, members of the woodpecker family, to dig holes in dead trees for their own nests. Once this task is completed the starlings make their move to fight and dispossess the flickers, sometimes hurling flickers' young to the ground. When spring arrived I would see many such battles. The starlings always won.

•   •   •

The wind swirled snow in the Central Park Zoo while a polar bear called Skandy paced up and down in his small cage, agitated. In the snow and cold, the bear looked one degree saner than he would appear in the high humidity of summer, when he seemed quite mad. A child leaned over the outer rail of the bear's cage and Skandy rushed at the bars, banging his head so a smudge of red showed on the ivory of his fur. Protective of his space, the giant carnivore had where humans live up to seventy-three thousand per square mile, and the lonely and frightened lock themselves voluntarily in their own cages.

•   •   •

There was panic in the Ramble. The blue jays' call of alarm sounded through the trees as a kestrel came in low and fast with a swoosh of wings. The sun reflecting off the snow dazzled me, but I could see two titmice scattering—the kestrel swerving around the sourgum holding the food containers, his head swinging from left to right to assess the situation. Then the kestrel saw me. He spread his pointed wings to give him lift and, using the momentum of his speed, brought himself clear of a red maple beyond the sourgum. Flapping hard, the raptor headed south, from where he had come, without looking back. I followed the kestrel through binoculars until he was a speck against the skyscrapers a mile away: the titmice, the chickadees, the nuthatches and the downy woodpeckers returned to feed.

It was seventeen days since I had seen the kestrel take the chickadee, and he had now learned there were easy pickings around the sourgum. It was a convenient place for me to observe a bird of prey going about his brutal business, and, keeping myself concealed, I saw both him and his much larger mate many times after that.

I did not have to see the dogs' urine freezing on Fifth Avenue to know the temperature had hit zero. The high-powered pooches of that neighborhood sported winter coats; some were made of leather and lined with fur, others were wool, depending on the owner's degree of affection and affluence. An elderly woman with gray hairs among the blue pulled a tissue from the pocket of her mink coat and bent to wipe her dachshund's backside, and on Dog Hill, off Fifth Avenue at Seventy-ninth Street, a poodle gamboled in the snow, ignoring his owner's command to start heading for home. The poodle's bright red coat was so large the dog looked more like a turtle. And creeping like a turtle, he would return to his owner and that human place outside the boundary of the park.

Two long lines of fifty Canada geese, the lines meeting at a point and the geese honking far off in the blue sky, passed over Dog Hill, heading farther south from a northwesterly direction. The geese were looking for fresh feeding grounds of grass and other vegetation not buried deep in snow. Most of the honking appeared to be coming from the leader of the flock and replies came from down the line. A few days later I saw another arrow of eighty geese. This time the leader changed position with another goose. The front-runner cuts through head winds and creates a slipstream to conserve the energy of birds flying behind him. Being out in front, though, is tiring work, and I surmised the noisy goose I had seen previously was complaining that it was someone else's turn to take over. It was tough where the geese had come from but the park's birds were constantly reminding me it was tough there, too.

In the area around the feeder tree, the birds were becoming incredibly tame. The cheekier titmice and chickadees were not alone in begging for food. A male cardinal came so close on an overhanging branch that I could have touched him. But, unlike the others, he refused to take a peanut from my outstretched palm. He simply jerked his black-chinned head downward, instructing me to throw the nut to the ground, but close to him so the blue jays would not steal it. I followed his instructions and with a "cheep" that was barely audible, the cardinal dropped into the snow to retrieve the nut. Two females gave me the same instruction, and all the while the chickadees and titmice tried to attract my attention by dropping level with my head before flying back to an adjacent branch.

The bond between man and the wild creatures sharing his immediate environment is cemented in that simple act of feeding a bird by hand. The birds, even if desperate for food, must be trusting and confident that this giant figure bearing gifts is also bearing good will. It is a thrilling, moving experience for the benefactor. The bird homes in so fast you flinch, thinking it will not stop and will career into you. Before you are fully aware of it, the bird is gripping your fingers with tiny, sharp claws. The chickadees usually grab the nut and fly off immediately but their relatives, the titmice, with crests erect in curiosity, pause for a moment to look you in the face.

•　　　•　　　•

The six species of gulls commonly seen on the reservoir during the course of the year are difficult to study. The gulls either swim in the center of the expanse of water, a good quarter of a mile from any vantage point, or, when the water is low, roost on a pipeline that stretches from a pumphouse at the northern end to one at the south. With the reservoir frozen over now, the gulls were beginning to gather in the hundreds near an open pool at the north end where fresh water arrives from holding reservoirs inland. As they bathed, the gulls were only about forty feet from the foot-path, and I decided this would be a good time to try to identify two of the less common winter gulls, the Iceland and glaucous species, which migrate from the far north of Canada and Greenland to winter on the eastern seaboard. During the next two months gull watching became my pre-occupation because I was determined to at least see the commoner Iceland species.

Two weeks after the arrival of the "Siberian Express" a slight rise in temperature caused the ice on the reservoir to thaw in places. Water surged from black cracks and the gull community scattered away from the pumphouse vantage point, making it difficult to observe them and dashing my hopes of seeing an Iceland gull that winter. Fifteen mallards were sheltering in the open space of water at the north end, coming and going from a feeding ground some-where outside Central Park. A lone canvasback male slept on the edge of the ice on January 25. When the gulls called excitedly, as they often did flying overhead, the canvasback did not bother to raise his head to look up. The duck had traces of oil on his underbelly and was in distress.

Although the reservoir ice was slowly thawing, temperatures barely climbed above freezing point for the rest of
January and snow continued to coat the park. In the Ramble,
squirrels begged for food after losing their hoards to the blue
jays. They would stand on hind legs, front paws tucked into
furry stomachs; and in the feeder area a squirrel accustomed
to a daily handout came up to me and prodded my boots
with his nose. It was while I fed the squirrel that the fabled
yellow-bellied sapsucker came into view.

If the sapsucker did not exist the people who satirize bird
watchers would invent it. The bird's quaint name is synony-
mous with stout boots and binoculars, with superenthusiasts
who appear out of step with a fast-paced world beyond the
gyr of the falcon, beyond parks' boundaries. The sapsucker
was the first I had seen and I thought he deserved better
than ridicule, although I cannot say the same for all bird
watchers. The bird embodied a subtle beauty—a yellow
wash to his belly and a splash of red on his black and white
patterned head. The species is easy to observe because it is
not as active as other woodpeckers. Instead of darting from
tree to tree, it prefers to stay put to drill neat lines of holes.
As its name suggests, it will return later to drink the sap
oozing from the holes and to eat insects attracted to it. This
particular bird spent forty minutes drilling a pine, all the
time sending flakes of bark and wood to the ground, like
falling snow.

•   •   •

The oiled canvasback looked in dreadful shape twenty-four
hours after I had first seen him. Forlornly, he paddled
through the water, his plumage without its usual sheen. At
the edge of the ice a black-backed gull dipped its head to
drink as the canvasback struggled to climb out of the water.
The drake pushed its chest onto the ice, tried to cock up its

left leg, slipped and plunged backward into the water. After several attempts the canvasback waddled ashore, a patch of oily, matted feathers visible. While in the water the duck had tilted its body to try to preen himself but he soon gave this up.

Canvasbacks, being estuarine ducks, spend much time out in New York City's bays, often falling victim to oil spills from coastal tankers. It was clear the oiled drake on the reservoir was dying, but life was going on about him. The three commonest gulls, the herring, the ring-billed, and the great black-backed, dunked their heads in the water, splashing and slurping. Suddenly they would leap from their bathing spot on strong wings, shake off the excess water while in mid-air and then come to a slippery halt on the ice. After a bout of preening, causing the ice to become coated with spent feathers, they would be off, clean and sparkling and ready for the filth and muck of the city's sewage outlets and garbage disposal sites.

The sun was warm, and I left the gulls to stroll down the east drive, to Dog Hill to look for an owl that had been making visits to the park. Beyond the hill was the frozen Conservatory Pond, known to many New Yorkers as the model boat pond, and on it a girl skated: a teenage girl in fawn beret and blue jersey and slacks, beautiful and willowy as she cut through the ice, twirling and jumping clear of the surface. Hans Christian Andersen, in bronze statue form, looked on, ignoring a squirrel running across his open bronze book. Nearby a bag lady slouched on a green wooden bench. She was the first bag person I had seen in the park during the month, although evidence of their encampments could be seen in hidden corners of the woods. The bag lady, a frown distorting her tanned, hairy face, wore a quilted coat over bulging woolens to keep out the cold. Layers of socks forced their way out of holes in the sides of her sneakers. The woman, surrounded by a suitcase and three shopping bags, started to swear at the girl who was skating, but the skater did not look up.

I climbed to the Point, a rocky promontory nudging into the boating lake, and for once felt claustrophobic in the park. The sharp early morning sunshine from over the East River cast the buildings all around in vertical lines of light and shadow, and this made them loom larger than they really were. From the Point, which faces due south, I could see the park in relation to the city: a narrow, fertile strip resisting concrete and glass. The air was clear and winter-fresh, seeming to draw the buildings even closer, their fine detail intensifying the newer skyscrapers like black and gold cigarette lighters standing on a rough-hewed table of oak.

•   •   •

The lone male canvasback which was coated with oil was dead within two days. His body had been dragged about forty yards by the gulls and now a greater black-backed gull was feeding on the carcass. The carelessness of someone handling oil meant the canvasback would not make it back to his breeding ground more than two thousand miles to the northwest. The gulls continued to stab at the carcass, and I knew it would not be the last oiled duck I would see during the year, nor the last carcass. The gulls also showed traces of oil pollution. Smudges of brown oil were evident on their bellies and underwings. I lingered at the reservoir, pondering how many ducks must be out in the bays and on the Atlantic Ocean suffering because of oil slicks, and thinking of the pure white beauty of the Iceland gull.

The bird watcher who had been so frosty at our first meeting seemed pleased to see me when we met, frequently now, on the reservoir footpath. Lambert and I constituted our own safety in numbers, even if that number was only two; and the ducks would have understood. Lambert had seen Iceland gulls on several occasions in January; his presence at the reservoir, his experience in identifying birds in flight, increased my chances of seeing the species. Many times we watched the arrival and departure, and the bathing ritual, of possibly a thousand gulls. It was gull traffic with a routine similar to the passage of aircraft arriving at La Guardia Airport, planes I could see constantly over the north end of the park. Because there was only a small patch of open water, the incoming gulls would wait in a holding pattern before spiraling down from great heights to make a perfect landing.

In late January, concerned that I was developing an obsession with gulls but still determined to see the Iceland species, I decided to spend one more complete afternoon at the reservoir. If I did not see an Iceland gull at this attempt I would give up searching for it, I told myself. I now had Lambert's telephone number and arranged to meet him on the reservoir footpath during the early afternoon of January 28.

I saw Lambert from a quarter of a mile away and recognized his profile immediately—hunched and squat like a patient heron at the reservoir's edge. Drawing closer along the path I could see the white beard running wild and wispy over the lower half of his face. Long white hair also flowed from under his hat so that it lapped at his collar, and the occasional puff of blue cigarette smoke ballooned above his head and sat momentarily in the heavy winter air. When I finally reached him, Lambert had bad news for me. He said he had been watching an Iceland gull for twenty minutes but it had taken off in the direction of the East River moments before I arrived. Again I laboriously checked the flock of gulls and could not tire of looking at them, or of seeing the dramatic spiral landing that brought the promise each time that the incoming bird might be an Iceland gull.

Lambert and I stayed all afternoon until a tired and

tarnished sunset sent a blade of amber light across the frozen reservoir, blunt and cold.

In the final days of January the number of gulls built up
dramatically. One morning I estimated two thousand gulls
were spread across the ice, and they were joined by two
black ducks—close relatives of the mallard—who were, no
doubt, struggling to find food like all the other dabbling
waterfowl.

The winter-white crispness of the year's first snowfall
had given way to a trampled, soiled coating of gray ice.
Footpaths formed a jagged terrain of hardened slush, but
frozen footprints, filling with water when the ice melted,
provided bathing tubs for the smaller birds.

On the last Saturday of January a white-throated sparrow took a footprint bath on the reservoir path and children
rushed by on their way to a winter carnival on the Great
Lawn. The children were lured by blaring music, which
featured snow-bells, and the downscale tinkle of the xylo-
phone creating a ripple effect that suggested falling snow. A
thousand pairs of cross-country skis, along with boots and
poles, had been laid down for the carnival. Around in circles
went a thousand pairs of feet to the rhythm of the music.
The children who were not skiing lingered at the site of an
ice sculpture contest; carved in compacted snow were a
female nude, a frog, and an alligator. Only the Iceland gull
was missing.

· *February* ·

It was on a sunny, crisp morning in early February that I first saw Billy. He ran along rough, cemented rocks that form the foundation for the wall at the back of the park's police station at the Eighty-sixth Street transverse. Billy could have been the cat in the "Tom Cat" California citrus advertisements of yesteryear: cold green eyes, wire-whiskers and big, rounded white patches on a glossy black coat. He had a house sparrow, still alive, in his mouth. Billy was the first feral cat I had seen in the park and I thought it was just a matter of time before he, like the other park cats, would be caught in one of the cat-catcher's traps, to be offered for adoption. At best to be sentenced to life in a New York apartment, at worst to be put down—whichever way you wanted to look at it. Billy (I still do not know why I gave him that name) had been surprised before he could kill and devour his catch, and he ran hard along the stone wall until it merged with the red brick above it, forcing him to jump two feet to the ground, and forcing a squeal from the sparrow. Billy stopped to glance back and when he realized I had also stopped to look at him, he broke into a loping cheetah run, crossing a patch of open space near the baseball diamonds at the top end of the Great Lawn. Gripping the sparrow harder, he vanished between a clump of pine trees.

•   •   •

The first of February brought a newcomer to the reservoir, an unusual duck for the park, a gadwall. A bird of fresh-water marshes, a dabbler who likes to hide in reeds, this gadwall must have been another victim of the "Siberian Express." The ice on the reservoir had now broken into drifts, exposing a large lake about one hundred yards long at the top end. The gadwall had arrived out of a blue sky during the mid-afternoon, and he joined two lesser scaups and a female ring-necked duck. The gadwall, mixing mottled gray and brown in its silky plumage, climbed from the water and promptly went to sleep on the ice alongside two mallards. Then the sound of a backfiring automobile spooked the mallards, and they shot into the air. The gadwall, smaller and lighter on the wing, went with them. The trio rose high to the east, making for the East River.

During the first week of February more gulls came to the park than at any other time in the year. There must have been three thousand gulls each morning on the ice, screaming and mewing and causing a general commotion. One morning, seeing the gray ice turned white with gulls, a jogger shouted to me as he passed, "It looks like an all-time convention . . . ," his words streaming behind him in freezing breath. I knew somewhere among this number must be an Iceland gull or a whole flock of them, and maybe even the glaucous gull. The cold, however, drove me home each morning after I could study only a fraction of the gulls' number. I gave the park a miss for a week in early February, trying to cure winter influenza and my obsession with seeing an Iceland gull. Clearing the mailbox for the first time in days I found a letter from Lambert. It was the first he had sent me, and I regarded the letter as a token of strengthening friendship. In it was a carefully drawn pen and ink sketch of a winter finch, a redpoll, he had found in the park.

"I could not reach you by phone," Lambert wrote. "But other winter birders made the scene. One lowered the gas on the gravy she was cooking and took a cab. . . ."

The redpoll is a rare bird for the park and, although the letter was a week old, I rushed to the location given, a patch of birch trees on the west side of the park. Within fifteen minutes I had reached the spot, determined to make this my thirty-fourth species of the year. I worked the birch trees for a distance of about ten blocks directly opposite the American Museum of Natural History, and I found three redpolls in a European silver birch near the open air Delacorte Theater. The redpoll breeds in northern Canada and comes south to feed, mainly pecking at the hanging seedpods of birches. The female tends to be a dull finch, but in this threesome was a fine male: red crown, black chin and pinkish breast. The birds leaped from branch to branch, clinging upside down at times to reach the tassels containing the seeds. I was fortunate to find the redpolls and I thought my luck might be in for an Iceland gull. It had been an oyster gray day and the light was dying quickly. But a fiery, orange sun prised its way through clustered shells of clouds, giving me time to reach the reservoir while the light was still good. A bird watcher I had not met before announced triumphantly that he had seen a good specimen of an adult Iceland gull. "It moved about ten minutes ago," he said with a smile.

•   •   •

A woman with flaming auburn hair partly hidden by a bright green woolen hat flapped her arms, leaped into the air and careered across the tarmac of the car park in front of the boathouse. The auburn hair, the green hat, a khaki winter coat and flowing fawn scarf were lost in a blur of movement and color as about forty birders tried to focus binoculars on the woman, who was now scuttling up a slight rise toward the Ramble. "Pretend I'm a blue jay," she shouted and about forty other people, without binoculars, giggled nervously. Lambert, sporting a feather from a great horned owl in a favorite bush hat, looked on approvingly and said to the crowd: "I have a new friend from overseas who says the blue jay's New York's bird. It's showy and noisy like all the people in the city."

The dance ritual, performed by a birder named Sarah, traditionally precedes the first of four bird tours during the year. The intention is to give bird watchers practice in focusing binoculars that have been put away for the winter. But the ritual also serves to turn the bird walk into one of the park's numerous happenings or events, occasions on which the outsider can penetrate a different layer or sphere of New York life; in this case, the cult of bird watching.

A thin, long line of heavily padded birders, and an equal number of people I suspected were going along to watch the bird watchers, took the winding path that leads to the Ramble, past a bag lady on a park bench who was airing her blankets in the sunshine. Like a subway train that stops abruptly, the line concertinaed at the feeder area, the first stop. The man who feeds the birds each winter, Bill Edgar, was raising replenished feeder bottles and cages, and he was pointed out to the walkers. Some raised binoculars for a closer look, even though he was only about twenty feet away.

"Bill feeds the birds out of his own pocket, so to speak," said Sarah, shouting so that the people crowded at the end of the line could hear. "Donations will be gratefully accepted." Quarters and the occasional dollar bill were pressed into Bill's hand. He then chased off a squirrel. "Got to give the birds a chance," he said, as he pointed out that the feeder containers were suspended by thin strands of wire to deter squirrels from climbing down to raid them.

The concertina stretched out again as the line headed

west over twisting paths, past a rustic shelter, through a stone viaduct and across the cast-iron bridge that crosses the Upper Lobe of the boat lake. Then the line stopped at the spot where the redpolls had been seen in previous days. "First time redpolls found in the park in four years," shouted Lambert but the birders without binoculars could not possibly see the four-inch-long finches in the tops of the birches. North went the birders and the concertina expanded and contracted here and there, emitting "oohs" and "ahs" as the more spectacular birds were seen; a cardinal here, a blue jay there. By the time the reservoir was reached, about a mile and a half from the walk's starting point, the concertina had shrunk considerably. And halfway around the reservoir it was only a third of its original length. Strangely, it was the people without binoculars who were remaining and I surmised it was Sarah's antics that kept them going on the bitterly cold day. Lambert, with a missionary zeal to promote the wonders of birds, was trying desperately to kindle interest among the uninitiated, but the reservoir proved a disappointment. We saw only a lone scaup and a batch of mallards, and we heard Lambert's accounts of the thrill of rarities like the tufted duck all the way from Europe, and the magic of the Iceland gull: "It's got snow-white mystique, it's the essence of. . . ." The arrival of a canvasback stopped Lambert in mid-sentence. The duck hit the water clumsily, completely immersing itself for a second in the splash, rising, shaking its head. The bird sailed uneasily for the edge of the ice and with a desperate leap, summoning all the strength it had, the drake hauled himself clear of the water and left a smudge of oil on the ice. The whole of the bird's white underbody was coated in black oil and the drake tugged at his feathers, trying to preen itself.

"He'll be dead by morning," said Lambert, and he looked away from the birders, remorseful that he should have showed them such a thing.

· · ·

By February 13 Chinese witch hazel started to bloom in a shady area behind the Cottage Puppet Theater on the west side. The witch hazel had tiny red flowers that promised the still far-off arrival of spring. All traces of the mid-January snowfall had melted now and a large tract of open water had split the ice on the reservoir in two. The vast numbers of gulls using the reservoir to bathe in early February had dispersed to other locations in New York City where fresh water had been released by the retreating ice. Many gulls had not made it through the cold spell and their bodies littered the reservoir surface where it was still frozen.

Crows had gathered at the Fifty-ninth Street end of the park, like vultures. They clung to the outer branches of an oak overlooking the Pond, a crescent-shaped area of muddy water that fits snugly into the corner of Fifty-ninth Street and Fifth Avenue.

Silently, without their familiar "caw," they looked down at a young, ring-billed gull. The bird, in second-year mottled juvenile plumage, stood on the ice gasping, dazed. It swung its head about slowly and two schoolboys, seeing the bird in trouble, walked to it across the solid ice that covered the Pond from shore to shore. The gull peered at them, reluctant to fly, but as they cautiously approached, the bird launched into the air in panic. Its right wing had been ripped off at the wrist, the joint where primary wing feathers begin. With one sound wing and half a wing flapping wildly, the bird swung around in circles. It appeared the gull had been attacked by a dog and the crows were impatient for it to die. After about fifteen minutes one of the flock took off on broad, black wings and flew over the gull, settling on the ice about forty feet away from it. The gull fixed the crow with beady eye, pulling back its head to raise a stout but sharp-tipped bill. The crow, however, had time on its side.

Sickened by crows and their summoning of doom, I left

the Pond and went north to the reservoir in another hunt for the Iceland gull. I needed the illusion of pristine lands, of tundra and nights like days, to take my mind away from the injured, dying gull. But instead of finding a bird of the far north among the thousand or so gulls taking their siesta and afternoon bath at the reservoir, I found a young black-backed shaking his head wildly. Stuck in this throat, and wrapped around his beak and head, was what appeared to be the plastic holder for a six-pack of beer. The plastic en-snarling the gull was part of the flotsam of winter piling up on the ice or in the water: a shattered green wine bottle spreading glass across the dirty ice, beer cans, broken beer bottles, a black umbrella turned inside out, a schoolbook—items that had been thrown or blown across the high fence. The gull was dead a few days later and the crows arrived first to pick at the carcass.

A horse was whinnying far away on the bridle path which runs between Turkey oaks in a wide circle around the reservoir. A rider, wearing traditional black equestrain cap, long black coat and polished boots with spurs, had pressed a bay into a gallop. The horse, steaming, came closer, and I noticed the bay and its rider were being watched by a silent, lonely figure I had often seen in the park. His head hidden in the hood of an anorak, the lone man stood under a pin oak on the west side in the Eighties, where he always stood. Sometimes the man had a home movie camera, sometimes not; sometimes he filmed, but I never deter-mined precisely what he was filming. No camera on this cold and gray day. He just watched the steaming horse as it pulled toward the warmth of the stables just off the park.

·   ·   ·

Officially it was still winter, but I could smell spring on February 15. An early morning silver sun brought temperatures to a high of fifty-seven degrees and the thawing ground released aromas of compost and humus: rich, sickly and sweet. There was another big concentration of gulls on the reservoir's ice and for a split second, in the blink of an eye, I thought I had seen the Iceland gull, a ghostly white shape among the grays and blacks of the other gulls. Before I could really study it, the bird vanished among the bickering, the preening and wallowing; a snowflake vanishing in a warm palm. I started to worry that my imagination might be running away with me. I had wanted to see this ethereal bird so much I may have been succumbing to fantasy. But it was an Iceland gull I had seen. I watched for another two hours, gave up, was heading out of the park, and then turned back for just one more look. In the long, central channel of open water between the ice floes I finally caught up with the bird. If I were an expert I could report that she—I like to think of the bird as female—was one of two subspecies that nests either in northeast Canada, or in Greenland. I could not determine the degree of gray in her wingtips that would identify her origin, as I watched her frolic in the water, pulling clear and then dunking her head again. She stretched lanky wings, shaking off droplets of water, and then flew away to join a group of herring gulls.

An unfamiliar sound rose off the reservoir, a sound that could not be drowned by the seaside cry of the herring gulls. A male canvasback let out a loud, resonant trill as he pursued a female through a maze of gulls. Because time for breeding is so short in the north-central United States and Canada, canvasbacks must court and pair in late winter so they can begin mating as soon as they arrive at their breeding grounds. The male scaups were soon to start wooing, too. But one bird would not make it north. Toward the end of February I saw the remains of a dead scaup, coated in oil, being buffeted against the wall of the reservoir.

•   •   •

"Man with large gun in the Ramble." The words were scrawled in the bird-sighting register at the boathouse and the regular park birders had formed a loose flock for protection. Lambert, now wearing a red-tailed hawk's feather in the band of his hat, led the way and most of the women in the group were tucked in tightly behind him. Lambert, a small but stocky man whom I estimated to be in his fifties, had grabbed a mugger with a gun a year previously in an unsuccessful attempt to wrestle the weapon away from the assailant. The mugger got away and Lambert now wished he could escape his reputation as Central Park's answer to the Guardian Angels subway vigilantes.

The birders defying the mugger as chickadees defy the blue jay at the feeder would not have missed anything if they had stayed at home on this dangerous day. The high-pitched whine of a power saw, accompanied by the crash of trees hitting the ground, had driven the winter birds out of the Ramble and a sharp odor of sap and chewed bark filled the air. Extensive tree-cutting had been ordered by the Central Park administration as part of a wider program to introduce more light to the Ramble's glades and to create vistas incorporated in the original, 125-year-old plan for the park. After the trees had been felled it was possible to observe two landmarks, Bethesda Fountain and the Belvedere Castle, from any position on a straight line between them. But many of the park users were not impressed. In the spring a petition protesting the tree-cutting would gather three thousand signatures. Sheared trunks and amputated tree limbs formed the backdrop for a conflict between tree lovers and the New York Parks Department that dragged on for most of the year.

· *March* ·

The girl who had been skating on the model boat pond in the last week of January was now out jogging. She bounced down the west side circular drive, heading south, and her slim, nimble body swayed to one side as she followed the gentle curve of the road. The piston motions of her arms forced her head from side to side, the sun catching her flaxen hair. The girl's face was ruddy and sweating, her red lips maroon with cold. She looked lanky and beautiful and as distant as the Iceland gull.

It had been some weeks since I had checked the bird sighting register in the cafeteria so on March 8 I took a stroll that way. As I flipped through the loose-leaf pages, I discovered that a long-eared owl had been sighted. The owl arrived in the park during late February and was still about, although birders had stopped giving its exact location because people were disturbing it. The last reported sighting was at Dog Hill; I headed to the area immediately. Knowing the owl would seek the densest cover possible, I scanned a clump of evergreens, looking for a foot-long elongated shape that might be pressed tight against a tree trunk for camoufl-age. I searched for an hour, covering perhaps sixty trees, and was about to give up when I saw what looked like two bird-ers standing under a pine at the top of the hill. They were kicking the tree and shouting at something in its branches. The fierce, orange eyes of the owl had given its hiding place away, although the mottled silver and brown of its feathers, two tufts like ears above the head, blended perfectly with the pine bark. The birders were trying to photograph the owl and wanted it to face into the sun. The bird, although looking in the opposite direction, obliged by slowly swinging its head in a semicircle, then winked an eye and bent its head to study the birders more closely.

Into the second week of March, nature's rebirth after winter was beginning in a profusion of swelling buds. Tiny yellow flowers bloomed on Eurasian dogwood trees and common grackles streamed into the park from areas immediately to the south of the city.

The glossy-plumaged grackles, wedge-tailed and about the size of a jay, took control of the feeder area. The smaller birds had to display a greater patience level because grackles have been known to kill other birds for merely getting in their way.

The birds, their fight for survival, their antics and trust of humans, had hooked me and during March I made a decision to visit the park daily for the rest of the year so I could study the birds over a complete twelve-month cycle. I determined that was the only way to observe them satisfactorily. I had started what birders call a checklist and I set a target for year-end—one hundred and fifty species—to give me an incentive to track down what might be in the park at any given time. I had hoped to record forty species by the end of February but had only made thirty-six. The month of March, however, with the spring migration gathering momentum, would give me a total of forty-seven.

Warm sunshine and temperatures rising to the upper fifties on March 12 brought wasps to the rubbish bins at the boathouse and a woodcock to the Upper Lobe of the boating lake, where willows began to sprout tiny shoots. The arrival of the woodcock traditionally signals the end of winter in the park, but I had decided my own harbinger of spring would be the American robin, a bird I had not seen during the winter. I knew of only one sighting—by Lambert in mid-February—and when I hurried off to find the bird, Lambert had shouted to me: "Remember one robin does not make a spring."

Now, on a patch of open ground between pin oaks, I came across three robins. Startled, the robins took off but the male among two females, pouting his orange breast, lingered on the low branch of a crabapple tree before dropping to resume feeding.

The boating lake and the fingers of gullies and streams, which feed it water from surrounding sections of the park, were edged by leafy willows by mid-March, the lime-green fringe contrasting sharply with the harsh brown of the other trees. It was in the willows that I saw the first important bird of spring, the Eastern phoebe. The species, a member of the tyrant flycatcher family, is the hardiest of the park's birds that prey on flying insects. The phoebe is easily identified because it stands upright on an exposed perch and, with a characteristic flick of the tail, launches into the air to hawk insects. I watched the bird for about half an hour and then followed it west across the circular drive, into a grassy gully, where it began to bathe in a stream. A song sparrow joined it, but both birds were disturbed by a vagrant who appeared from the holly bushes. He placed a sleeping bag and two canvas grips alongside a big rock, which was partly obstructing the flow of water. The hobo took off his shoes, peeled off his socks and threw the socks into a pool. He reached into one of the grips, took out what appeared to be some more socks, underclothing, and a cake of soap. He had come to do his washing.

Near the sea lion enclosure, in the zoo, a man who

dresses as a clown and calls himself Pegasus was telling a group of children: "Now stand back everyone and I'll give you each a magic wand. . . ." Skandy, the polar bear, was in the open section of his enclosure but the big cats were still locked in their cramped, heated winter quarters. A tiger cub, mischief in its wide yellow eyes, took swipes at a log, pretending it was prey to be killed. Six months later Skandy would do likewise, but he would have a man trapped between his powerful claws.

•   •   •

The loud rattle of a kingfisher startled two newly emerged turtles at the boating lake on March 20, and they slid from their log back to the caress of the mud. The female belted kingfisher settled in a willow near the boathouse and, after a few seconds, was off again, heading the five blocks to the Hudson River. The species is described as "belted" because the female has a large chestnut band across her chest, something lacking in the male. The female, in fact, is more gaily colored than the male, a rare characteristic in eastern America's species. I saw a male a little later and, when he heard the female calling from above Broadway, he soon headed in the direction of the Hudson.

A pair of flickers arrived on golden wings that same afternoon and within a few days there were hundreds more, some to spar with the starlings over nesting sites. The starlings, in their aggressive moments, resemble prize fighters: stocky, heads hunched in shoulders. Although bigger and with longer bills, the flickers were out of their class in these bouts.

A mourning cloak butterfly zigzagged along a Ramble footpath as a crow gathered nesting material. The butterfly came to rest on a rock and splayed out its broad, chocolate wings, edged with yellow. The crow building the nest had gathered what looked like dead leaves in its bill, but before the bird could get to the nest site, high in a pine, a pair of grackles mobbed it. The grackles had chosen the same tree for their nest; they lunged at the crow, unable to defend itself because of the leaves in its beak. Finally, the crow struck back and bowed its head to see the leaves flutter to the ground. Lazily, as if not to create the impression it was making a retreat, the crow moved out of the tree and did not return to complete the nest.

•   •   •

The words were still falling from my lips when I realized it had been a mistake to utter them. I was addressing the vagrant I had seen washing his socks a few days earlier. The man, clutching a quiet dignity along with his grips, asked me for a quarter and I said curtly: "Go find yourself a job."

I did not think of the implications, or the callousness of such a remark, and what followed was a dissertation on the worst economic crisis the United States had experienced since the Great Depression of the 1930's, although the vagrant could not have remembered those times. He appeared to be in his mid-thirties, around the same age as I, and did not fit the usual description of a bag person, whatever that might be.

"Do you know there are millions of people out of work? Tell me how to find a job and I'll take it," he said, and I felt ashamed.

•   •   •

The mourning cloak butterfly had promised spring but another cold front moved over New York City in the final days of March. It was so cold a foot-long stalactite of frozen sap hung from the branch of a birch that had been machine-gunned by a sapsucker. Two laughing gulls returned from winter playgrounds as far south as Florida on March 26 to find ice at the edge of the reservoir and the carcasses of more winter gulls—gulls which had succumbed to the cold. But this did not deter the laughing gulls from engaging in courtship displays way out in the center of the reservoir. The male thrust at the female to attract her attention, then took off and flapped as high as the Fifth Avenue rooftop gardens. With half-folded wings he plummeted, finally stretching out wings and feet to make a pelican landing, with a splash, next to his female.

Checking the register in the late afternoon, I found a migrating wood duck and a rarer blue-winged teal listed. With only twenty minutes of sunlight left I had to quickly decide between trying to find the wood duck on the boating lake or running to the reservoir to see the teal. I knew the wood duck, a dabbler in shallow water, could well be hidden in a lobe and take hours to find. At least I would be able to pick out the teal quickly, I reasoned. So I hurried to the reservoir, past Dog Hill and the canines with their winter coats back on, past joggers going home before it became dark. The usual flotilla of scaups and ruddy ducks, dozing in the sunlight, was spread across the reservoir, but I could not see the teal, a small bird whose wintering ground stretches from Florida down to Peru. I carried on walking, nervously, because the footpath was deserted, and I was at the spot where I had been mugged nearly three months previously. After glancing behind me, I focused my binoculars on a dark dot on the water, and there was the teal, a fine male. I had two minutes of setting sun to study his dark, bluish plumage; a distinctive narrow crescent of white curving from his forehead to below his chin, a streak of light blue on the wing. The sun dropped behind the tall buildings on the West Side, which hung like jagged cliffs over the park. At the precise moment the buildings' shadows raced across the reservoir, the teal pranced from the water and flew fast and low toward the flotilla, landed and nestled among the scaups.

· · ·

"Quack, quack," said the old man who was swirling around the Loeb boathouse cafeteria on roller skates. He wore a red checked jacket, bright red pants and attached to a false pink nose were false glasses and a false moustache. The cafeteria was crowded but the only person paying attention to the old man, gray hair poking from under a Yankees baseball cap turned back-to-front, was a little girl of about five. "Quack, quack," said the roller skater to the girl, who replied coldly: "You look silly. . . ."

"Well, you can't win 'em all," said the old man, looking hurt. He turned slowly and skated out of the cafeteria.

Red maples bloomed during the last weekend of March and squirrels ran through the branches of the trees to chew at the orange and red flowers. Stripped twigs littered the ground beneath the trees and a roller skater cursed when his skates stopped at the obstruction and he did not. At the Point another spring migrant, the golden-crowned kinglet, had arrived, and a pair of these birds worked a clump of black cherry bushes, looking for insects.

The birds were oblivious to danger, but danger lurked. A female kestrel was perched at the end of the Point and she had her eyes on the kinglets. The small birds were slowly moving toward the sourgum with the kestrel in its branches. I moved at the same pace behind them. Sometimes they were only a few feet in front of me, but they remained unaware of me or the kestrel. We were close to the kestrel now and the bird of prey focused on me. Wary, she nudged into the wind and was off. Within a few minutes I was to see my third bird of prey of the year. Peering into a cloudless sky, a raptor came into view a hundred feet above me. It was a red-tailed hawk, pretty common in the New York area, and it soared in wide circles that took it over both Central Park West and Fifth Avenue on each complete sweep. The thermals lifted it higher and the hawk, on rounded wings with fingers of feathers at the tips, sailed out of sight.

Although all raptors are superb flyers, the falcons are the masters of the air and even such dartlike birds as the barn swallow and chimney swift are not safe from aerial attack. The falcons are tailored for speed, but it is not only their tapered wings which separate them from the larger buteo and accipiter hawk species as well as the eagles, owls and vultures. Falcons have relatively weak talons and do not use them to pierce and kill their prey the way other hawks and owls do. Instead, falcons rely on powerful jaw muscles and short, compact beaks to bite at the neck of victims, killing them instantly. Female falcons are also much larger than males and scientists believe the reason for this may be that a larger female is more likely to produce a greater number of surviving offspring.

The notable falcons of the New York City area are the gyrfalcon and the peregrine, both particularly rare, for different reasons. The gyrfalcon, the largest and most powerful of its family, sometimes assuming a virtually pure white plumage, is a bird of arctic North America, Europe and Asia and winters infrequently in the northern United States. The peregrine, reputed to reach speeds of two hundred miles per hour in its drive or "stoop" for prey, has virtually been wiped out as a nesting bird in the eastern United States because of its susceptibility to poisoning by persistent pesticides. It was the decline of the peregrine that alerted many governments worldwide to the dangers of the chemical DDT. A buildup of DDT in aquatic creatures ranging from fish to ducks formed in higher concentrations in the bodies of birds preying on them. Peregrines commonly feed on waterfowl—another name for them is "duck hawk"—and the concentration of harmful chemicals caused a thinning of the shells of their eggs, and ultimately, the peregrine's inability to rear young.

Since the banning of DDT, the peregrine has begun to make a gradual comeback and young birds, reared in captivity, have been released in New York City in the hope that they will return to breed in aeries on high-rise buildings, as they have done in the past.

·   ·   ·

Lambert had been feeding the birds in the park since wintering species like the chickadees arrived in October and November of the previous year. Through the winter months his pockets bulged with packets of unshelled peanuts and at least one of the chickadees grew to recognize Lambert. This particular bird had a touch of albinism in the tail and was easily identified. I saw the bird many times, but it would not come to me directly unless I actually pursued it and littered the ground with peanuts to attract its attention. When, however, I was with Lambert I noticed the bird sought us out and made a beeline for the nearest branch overhanging Lambert's bush hat. The bird, with a noisy *chick—a—dee—dee—dee,* told Lambert what it wanted and flew to his hand without fear.

Lambert, longsighted like a hawk, found two more Iceland gulls on consecutive days at the end of March. He pointed out they were of the Kumlien sub-species, from Canada. A month earlier I would have been excited by the gulls but I had become blasé now, my fresh target being the woodcock. On March 31 I decided to spend the whole day looking for a woodcock, starting out at the southern lobe of the boating lake where one had been seen the day before. The night-flying woodcocks often overfly the city when they have strong tailwinds and their sightings in Central Park are relatively uncommon. My hopes of seeing a woodcock at the boating lake location were dashed because a dapper young man, in three-piece suit, was under a nearby wooden pavilion, trumpet in hand, facing a chrome stand holding sheet music. "Somewhere Over the Rainbow" started to boom out over the lake as I watched for a woodcock in flight. I could understand why the trumpeter was practicing in the park. His neighbors, no doubt, had complained about his music—those missed notes and long pauses for breath. A little later, still hunting for a woodcock, I came across an aspiring actor in a long tweed coat, learning his lines. Studied pose, assertive voice; three blocks and a world separated him from Broadway.

I failed to find a woodcock but amid rusting beer cans, in a boggy area, I discovered another new bird, a swamp sparrow. The sun had enticed a solitary daffodil to unfurl its flower in the Shakespeare Garden and the year's second mourning cloak butterfly fluttered around flowering crocuses. The crocuses would have been enough to complete a perfect day of wildlife study but there was one more surprise. Out on the boating lake were two bufflehead ducks, a male with a bonnetlike white patch on his dark head, and his chocolate brown female. They had sought shelter in a creek from the choppy waters and were out of sight of the skyscapers and park paraphernalia of statues and pavilions and benches. I thought for a moment of the untamed wilderness that greeted the first Europeans to North America, a land to be drained of fifty percent of its wetlands, to be stripped of much of its forests. The puffy head of the male bufflehead looked to the pioneers like the head of the then common buffalo, and that is why the species was given its name.

The bufflehead departed for Canadian breeding grounds as mourning doves completed a twiggy nest in a black cherry tree overlooking the boating lake. And, on the last night of March, the first thunderstorm of the year rolled across the sky.

· *April* ·

*I*t's April Fool's Day but I won't be playing any jokes, it's tough enough living in New York City as it is." The comment came from a disc jockey on an early morning radio show, but Gordon Davis, the Commissioner of the New York City Parks Department must have thought someone was playing a prank on him. From behind the curtains in his office overlooking the sea lion pond in the zoo, he looked down at about thirty people carrying placards and shouting slogans. Among the crowd were parks staff in plain clothes, making conversation with walkie-talkie radios. Mr. Davis, it appeared, was getting the message.

"It's a bunch of cranks," said a young man on roller skates to his girlfriend, but Lambert and Sarah were too busy shouting to hear the remark. They were part of a demonstration to protest the spraying of the city's parks to eliminate gypsy moths. The insects were imported by a French naturalist more than a century ago in an attempt to cross-breed them with silkworms to produce a disease-resistant strain. The experiment failed, and some of the caterpillars escaped. The gypsy moth has blighted indigenous elms and other species of trees across the eastern United States ever since. Central Park was not part of the program to spray four city parks with a chemical pesticide, but the protesters said the chemical would be dangerous to the health of all New Yorkers, and would decimate populations of native butterflies and insects as well as the birds that prey on them.

A larger confrontation with the Parks Department over the cutting of trees in Central Park was also developing and the demonstration in front of the Parks Department office served as a rallying cry for this protest, too.

I arrived early for the demonstration and killed time by walking to the Pond at Fifty-ninth Street. Scanning the mallards that make the lake their permanent home, when it is free of ice, I caught a glimpse of something bright and multicolored plopping into the water from the far bank. It was a male wood duck, the most spectacular duck species in North America. When I reached the nearby zoo I told Lambert about my find and his face brightened under his hat, which had a blue jay's feather tucked into it. Then his face clouded with apprehension. "Don't tell the other birders yet," he said. "They'll desert the demo." Studying the wood duck for a half hour, I had considered it too exotic for that muddy pool; it belonged in a zoo where everyone could see its beauty. But the folly of that sentiment struck me once I was back in the zoo. A wood duck stood dejectedly in a cage with a concrete floor. Two African gray parrots, looking more at home on a wooden perch, kept the duck company. The drake's feathers lacked the wild male's splendor and he looked so dull he could have been a female. He would never attract a mate in that condition, in or out of the zoo. He would not be part of the mating ritual, or part of the migration; of moonlit flights covering a continent, of landing in far-flung muddy places; wary of alligators in winter and, in summer, defending young against attack from night herons.

The nocturnal herons, I would later discover, are the biggest predators of ducklings in the park. Two of the herons arrived on southerly winds on April 2; they stood sentinel in the Ramble, perched in the branches of a pin oak.

The black-crowned night heron, found in every continent except Australasia, has a sinister appearance to comple-
ment a sinister, even macabre nature. At dusk the herons
sweep like vampire bats from their high perches to feed at
lake and river margins, snapping up a variety of prey from
fish and frogs to the young of other birds. Even in bright
sunlight the tall birds cut a ghostly shape in gray plumage,
a spiny black crest jutting from the back of their heads.

The arrival of the night herons added spice to the pot-
pourri of species that came to the park, but the interest of
the birders was mainly focused on the warblers, a family of
small, brightly colored insect-eaters. April and early May is
warbler time in the park. Birders do not need a calendar
during normal, seasonal weather to establish what week of
the year it is. They can determine approximate dates by
observing which of the thirty-two warblers consistently
sighted in the park is in town. The first warbler to arrive is
usually the pine warbler, a drab species compared to the
other forty eastern members of the family. The pine warbler, usually found in conifers, winters from a line not too far
south of New York City and so has a head start on its cousins,
whose winter ranges can reach the Amazon Basin and Argentina. I searched for the pine warbler among the pines on
Dog Hill but only found a hobo living there, a man I called
the "pine person." The vagrant had made a two-foot-high
bed of pine needles in the fall and had lived under the pine
trees all winter. He rolled out of dirty blankets when he saw
me coming and kicked aside an empty bottle of cheap bourbon.

"Get away," he said hoarsely, fighting to squeeze the
words from a mouth burned dry by the spirit, and I moved
away to the Conservatory Pond where the first miniature
yachts of the year were jostled by the wind. A crowd always
gathers at the pond to watch the enthusiasts guide crafts
around buoys, the "skippers" changing the pitch of sails and
the angle of rudders by means of signals from radio transmit-

ters. A hobbyist, as jealous as any other park user of his corner of the park, had encountered an unexpected hazard: a male wood duck was resting on the pond. At first the owner of the white-sailed ship paid little attention to the duck, although a birder ran to the boathouse cafeteria to announce the waterfowl's arrival. Soon a bigger crowd than normal on a weekday was gathering on the concrete path around the lake and the boat owner, at first, thought the birders were admiring his sailing craft. Then he considered the bird might in some way be controlled by the bird watchers because the drake made a beeline for the boat, barging it and swamping it with water. Desperately, the enthusiast twiddled the knob of his radio transmitter to tack into the wind and guide the craft to safety. The duck pursued the boat, however, and when he caught up with it, he lifted a webbed foot to climb aboard, capsizing the craft and submerging its sails. The drake then sprang into the air and took off. And the birders also beat a hasty retreat.

•   •   •

The willows were now fully in leaf. Fresh green sprouts sprinkled the crab apple trees but soft snow flurries on April 4 were a stinging reminder that winter was reluctant to recede. Hundreds of the winter sparrows had gathered in the park from the south, wary about moving on to areas where there might be worse weather. The lowest temperature reading of the day touched freezing point and on the Point a cottontail rabbit moved slowly, cranking its stiff limbs. Next day heavier snow fell in a diagonal windblown pattern across the reservoir, and the weathermen warned that a freak April blizzard was on its way.

Three A.M., April 6. The snow started again and in the next thirteen hours a foot of snow was dumped on the city, making it the worst April blizzard in New York's history.

The thermometer also fell to twenty-one degrees, its lowest April level since records were started more than one hundred years previously. The snow brought chaos to the city and the circular drive in Central Park had to be closed after a series of accidents involving taxis. I was out in the park at first light and dodged a man on cross-country skis, who was trudging around the reservoir footpath. Falling snow clogged the wire-mesh fence. Shaking this away, I saw five ruddy ducks, hunched into the wind with snow on their backs. On the footpath a robin struggled to find food. I moved closer and the robin did not make an effort to fly. When I was about three feet away he merely hopped to one side to let me pass, vanishing momentarily under the snow. Robins feed mainly on insects and worms, but later in the day one of the species would be forced to deviate from his normal diet and beg a peanut. The insect-eating birds that had arrived prematurely from the south were in serious trouble. At the Loeb Boathouse a phoebe huddled at the base of a sloping rock, picking up insects that also sought shelter.

Against the back wall of the police station, where I had first seen Billy, fox sparrows and juncos found comradeship and solace in the knowledge they had been wise enough not to move farther north. I had gone to the wall to find Billy. In a knapsack I had a carton of milk and some beef jerky, along with several packets of peanuts for the nut and seed-eating birds. After searching for Billy for an hour, I poured milk into a plastic saucer and put out the jerky just in case he should happen by, though I knew even in this severe weather he would not be endangered. From fleeting glimpses of him, I could see Billy was lean but fit, his coat healthy, a sparkle in his eyes. The snow posed a problem of camouflage, however. Billy's black coat would work against him, betraying his stealthy advance on vulnerable birds, but he could hole up for a day, waiting for the worst to pass, being smart, licking the snow for moisture and just getting a little leaner.

The freak blizzard had brought another phenomenon, thunder above the snow. Two storm systems, from both north and south, had collided over New York City; and if the Algonquin Indians had still been crossing Manhattan by an Indian trail, which is now named Broadway, they would have thought the gods were particularly angry on this strange day. The storm had killed many of the birds in the park. I came across the bodies of two robins and a flicker, and I stopped to pick up a feeble phoebe, his wings drooped in despair. He died in my hand, his body warm and limp. The ground was too hard to dig him a grave so I placed him alongside the jerky and plastic saucer; an offering not to the gods, but to Billy.

Already I was half an hour late for work. I would have to hail a taxi on Fifth Avenue. Taxis were moving slowly, but finding an empty one was a problem. After about ten minutes I made out the shape of an empty taxi, and I leaped up and down to attract the driver's attention through the blizzard. Hunched over the steering wheel, the driver caught sight of me and pulled to one side of the road—only to run into a two-foot drift of snow piled up against the sunken curb and a fire hydrant. The driver tried to back out but the wheels of the cab spun, digging deeper into the snow. Hanging my binoculars over the hydrant, I started to push the cab but I slipped and vanished into the snow. I rose looking like a snowman but the driver was not amused. He had to abandon his cab and, standing alongside me at the junction of Fifth and Seventy-ninth Street, he found he had competition for the first cab.

"Hey jerk," said the driver after a few minutes, "you go find yourself annoyder coyner."

When I returned to the park the next day the tracks of a cat, a small cat, the size of Billy, led to and from the plastic saucer. The jerky and the body of the phoebe had disappeared, and Billy stared at me from some loose rocks behind a children's playground a hundred yards from the police station wall. He turned slowly to retreat into a crevice, which I determined to be his lair, but he was nervous, glancing back at me and not wanting to give his hiding place away. I moved slowly in his direction, calling his name, slowly, stretching the vowel, stressing the last syllable, the way you would for a child. He turned and ran.

·   ·   ·

Even in winter, when it is not shrouded by the weeping branches of willows, you have to search hard to find the Indian Cave. The cave hides under a cliff of Manhattan schist, the cold gray stone forming the park's bedrock, and it endeavors to keep its secret to itself. The park's designers had intended a grotto to serve their Victorian romanticism in the Ramble but the Indian Cave remains a cave. Somehow, the word *grotto* has a human connotation, which does not apply in this case. The entrance to the cave is protected by a thirty-yard patch of mud, which sweeps in a crescent from deep in the Ramble to the boating lake. A footpath, hemmed against the top of the cliff by a guard rail, crosses above the cave but does not betray its location. Reaching the cave is not easy, even when you know where it is. You must edge along the base of the cliff, your feet sinking into the mud. Once you have moved halfway around the crescent, you have the mouth of the cave in sight and are looking at another, wetter, blacker patch of mud, which is soaking up water trapped by a fallen willow. It was in this wetter, blacker patch of mud that I looked for the woodcock.

It seemed certain the blizzard of the previous day, during the dark hours of the morning, could have forced night-flyers down, and no bird would try to move on at this critical

time. Rounding the promontory that shelters the Indian
Cave from the boating lake, I slowed and edged my way
carefully for fear of flushing the shy species. A bird with a
long bill took flight and zigzagged around me, vanishing
around the promontory. I determined this was my bird.
Turning to pursue it, another bird with long bill swept by on
rapid wingbeats and this one looked markedly different. The
confusion had me consulting my bird identification book,
and I could not establish if I had seen a woodcock or a snipe,
or both. The dread of birdwatchers is to see something special for a moment and not be given a second look at it. But
I was not to be beaten. I ran around the promontory and
immediately put up a snipe, which now flew to the west side
of the boating lake, landing and merging with a rock in
perfect camouflage. The snipe, although a much more slender bird than the chunky woodcock, is mainly identified by
its white eye stripe and chestnut coloring in the tail. This
specimen started to probe in the mud and again it was only
its erratic movement that gave its mottled plumage form
and shape against its background. But the camouflage of the
snipe could not match the woodcock's when I finally found
the second bird I had flushed.

I had moved along the lake shore to the Upper Lobe,
about a hundred yards north of the Indian Cave, at the
northernmost point of the lake. Sliding down the snow-cov-
ered steep bank that leads to the water, I steadied myself
against a small oak. Two willows shelter the lobe and the
snow had melted under them, exposing black mud where
the leaves of countless falls were decomposing. At the edge
of the mud, in front of a wall of snow, I caught the silhouette
of a stumpy, neckless bird, which I knew to be a woodcock.
The leaflike pattern on its head and back showed up clearly,
giving explanation to hunters' stories of woodcocks remaining unseen until they were virtually underfoot. The woodcock moved away from its white backdrop after a little while

as melting snow fell from the overhanging willows and plopped into the water. The woodcock was not alone. I was only about twenty yards away but I had to look through field glasses, carefully, to see five more woodcocks squatting in the mud. The woodcocks were to move out that night, which was clear and sprinkled with stars, but the snipe lingered for a few days, even pausing to pick at worms in the mud of the Azalea Pond, at the heart of the Ramble's maze of paths, its busiest human junction.

The intricately winding paths of the Ramble, cutting through thick forest, actually make the area appear larger than it is. The park's designers, Frederick Law Olmsted and Calvert Vaux, planned it that way and never intended it to be an exact re-creation of a natural wilderness, because they introduced Druidic and Gothic romanticism of the nineteenth century in the form of the rustic arch with its narrow, elongated opening, the Indian Cave, and the Belvedere Castle.

In recent years, a Ramble glade was dubbed "mugger's wood" by the birders to indicate the violent reality of city life in the twentieth century, and the dangers of the Ramble were heightened by its reputation as a gathering and meeting place for members of New York's male gay community. In less tolerant times the Ramble attracted provocateurs intent on violence against the homosexuals. Now the danger comes from muggers seeking out people who might be male prostitutes, on suspicion they are carrying large sums of money.

"The gays don't trouble us and we don't trouble them," Lambert said when he first took me around the park, explaining an example of coexistence that saw the gay and bird watching fraternities fusing in a mutual understanding: the two groups watch out for each other and provide a combined force against the incursions of muggers.

Although designed with humans in mind, the Ramble is

also an important crossroads for bird species in winter and early spring, mainly because of the feeder tree situated at its center. And the kestrel was not alone in discovering that the feeding activity made the area fertile mugging territory. There was another, unexpected predator; Billy had moved into the neighborhood. Every now and then I caught a flash of black and white, silky fur and motion, a captured image of the protagonist of the Tom Cat advertisements of yesteryear. Billy was somehow wilder than any of the other animals in the park; without trust, without inclination to return, submissively, to the dominant beings who took his ancestors from the wild, eons ago, and gave them a semblance of domesticity. I wanted to be friends with Billy but I doubted that would ever be.

·　　·　　·

Three days after the blizzard more snow fell briefly, but the birds, at least, had decided winter was finally over. The woods, although twisted and bare in the tortured shape of winter, were filled with song. Some birds would throw back their heads in violent movement to hit the highest note. Others, like the blue jay, were casual about singing, if you could call the noises they uttered a song at all. The worst noise came from the grackles, a grating, croaking sound.

In dribs and drabs other migrant species were arriving, to precede the rush of warblers and the other perching, insect-eating birds of summer. In the Indian Cave a winter wren stayed for a few days, and fish crows were chased by grackles who thought the smaller relatives of the common crow might be thinking of setting up home near their communal nesting sites.

Into the third week of April the build-up to spring was back on course. Temperatures were at a seasonal average but plant growth, which had been literally nipped in the bud, was at a standstill, stunted by the blizzard. Sunshine encouraged strollers to strip down to shirt-sleeves and T-shirts; and, on Dog Hill, the "pine person" had vacated his bed and now soaked up the sun like a turtle. He lay on his back with bare feet propped on two suitcases. Beside him, battered and beaten boots, laced with string, lay with their toes pointing together on the grass. The "pine person," a man in his sixties, was killing time before taking to the streets of the Upper East Side to raid garbage bins. Ostensibly, he was free of our consumer culture's dictate to work and spend, but he had his daily routine, nonetheless. He would only leave the park during the late afternoon, after garbage bins emptied in the morning had started to fill up again. His working day finished at about 9 P.M., when he drifted back to Dog Hill. One day I saw him sharing a half loaf of stale bread with pigeons. The gesture had an unintended symbolism because many birders regard town pigeons as the "bag people" of the avian world. The feral pigeon is descended from the rock dove of Europe, a bird that traded its speed and homing instinct for a dry pigeon coop and regular food in the service of man. The rock dove's plumage of slate-gray and black with a green iridescence in the neck feathers, can still be seen in many of the selectively bred, bastardized feral pigeons. I don't know how the park's pigeons arrived in America. But somewhere between the rugged cliffs of Europe and accepting a hand-out of stale bread in Central Park, they lost their way and, like the man feeding them, they too ended up on the streets of New York City.

·   ·   ·

What is thought to be America's most prolific land bird, the red-winged blackbird, sang heartily from the reeds skirting the Belvedere Lake on April 12, a few days after his cousin, the rusty blackbird, had shared a patch of mud with a woodcock. The red-wings form southern roosts with other family members in winter, which can number millions of birds, but they do not generate much interest during the spring in Central Park. Spring, the birders will remind you, is warbler time. In April the hunt is on for the first warblers of the migration. Someone had already seen a pine warbler; but the other early arrivals, the palm warbler and the Louisiana waterthrush, had yet to make an appearance.

Lambert was sporting his spring birding outfit, a denim jacket and khaki pants, on April 15. He had a grackle's feather tucked in his hat; he vowed he would find one of the three warblers before the day was out. Lambert had a jauntiness about him, a quickness of pace, and the strengthening sun of spring had given a red flush to his face so it showed no lines to indicate his age. His eyes were blue and clear, and they led him away from the Ramble, because half a century of springs had taught him that the Ramble was not the place to find the first warblers.

I had been out for five hours and had enough of this fruitless warbler chase for the day. But after fifteen minutes in the boathouse cafeteria, I succumbed and went in search of Lambert, who had headed in the direction of the Belvedere Lake. The palm warbler seemed the best bet for the day, being the commonest of the early trio. The species winters in the southern United States, and its name is largely erroneous; the palm warbler seldom feeds in palms but prefers the floor of deciduous forests during migration, and likes boggy areas in its breeding range in southern Canada. Lambert was sitting, smugly, on a bench on the south side of the lake. Behind him, amid dead beech leaves, was a small yellowish bird with a chestnut cap—a palm warbler.

The entry in my diary read: "Spring arrived on April 16, sunny, warm—temperature seventy degrees." A log in the boating lake, which had been coated with snow just nine days previously, now had two species of turtle on it, a red-eared turtle and a diamondback. Neither of these species are indigenous to the park but have been placed in the lakes and ponds after outliving their novelty as pets, growing too large for apartment tanks. The red-eared turtle was more than a foot long and in the coming months I would see it mate. But the turtles would not be able to propagate because the park is without suitable sand in which the turtles can bury eggs. The six species of turtles, including the park's indigenous snapping turtles, would have to rely on the pet trade to keep their species represented in the heart of the city.

On the southerly winds bringing warm air from Florida, a deluge of migrating birds was awaited. Two weeks ahead of the warbler timetable came a blue-winged warbler, making the Point his home for ten days while he allowed the rest of his species to catch up with him. On schedule was the Louisiana waterthrush, to be followed quickly by ground-feeding birds of different species that had not moved north until they were sure the thaw was for real. These were the rufous-sided towee and the brown thrasher, a relative of the mockingbird which, despite a mad look in its yellow eyes, is one of the loveliest birds of the woods. Next to arrive was the northern waterthrush as preparations for the nesting season began, and the woods were a frenzy of activity. A blue jay flew by, struggling with a ten-inch stick, which would form the main support of a heavy nest. And in a nearby beech, a male and female jay squabbled on a slender branch. Then the birds touched beaks tenderly—a ritual I saw performed by many of the park's nesting birds—before the female spread her wings in submission and lay her body low along the branch so the male could climb on her back.

The avian activity coincided with an explosion of small leaves and flowers, although, in an overview, the park retained the bare, bleak appearance of winter with splashes of whites and greens dotting the branches. Pink cherry blossoms attracted the first bee of the spring, and a flicker I had seen scouting nesting sites near the boathouse cafeteria called for a mate to join him. There was competition of a different kind for the robins, some of whom had found a patch of grass near the boating lake, which was alive with hundreds of worms. Little boys with fishing rods had discovered this area as a source of bait; when the boys arrived the robins had to move out. The fishermen brought an unexpected bonus for the robins, though. Discarded fishing line made ideal nest material, and many times I would see a robin trailing a length of line to its nest. Binding twigs, leaves and moss with the nylon line made the nests indestructible to everything but the schoolboys, who would later be bent on their destruction.

The next birds to arrive came in bulk. Hundreds of blue-gray gnatcatchers, relatives of the kinglets, flooded into the park in mid-April. They could be seen in virtually every tree, creeping through the treetops like feather-tailed mice in search of insects. On the forest floor there was a similar invasion of hermit thrushes. Within a week this phase of the migration would be over, only the occasional gnatcatcher or thrush being caught in the surge of the next species to hit the park.

A change in wind direction, from the south to north, appeared to halt the migration on April 18, but there was a migration of a different kind, which came from the streets. With the blossoming of spring, less hardy New Yorkers, who had shunned the park in winter, re-discovered its beauty, and hundreds of thousands of people made for its two-and-a-half-mile openness. Bird song was drowned by the heavy, thudding beat pulsating from music systems. Conflicting rhythms from Jamaican steel drums and Puerto Rican skin instruments reverberated across the boating lake; under a statue of Polish warrior King Jagiello, at the Belvedere Lake, folk dancers gathered, as they do every weekend during the spring and summer and early fall. Central Park has an estimated fifteen million visits by three million people each year, the biggest crush occurring in the early spring. Crime also rises at this time and neighboring police precincts transfer officers there, to boost the permanent force at the Central Park stationhouse.

I had now seen sixty-three species of birds and was awaiting what birders call a "wave day" to increase my total. The bird watchers now made a daily note of the wind direction, looking for a south-westerly wind, which followed storms, or for strong winds coming from the north. Migrating birds mainly travel on southerly winds in spring. Although headwinds might not hamper them unduly, gales and storms force the birds to hold tight wherever they are until the wind changes direction. If there is persistent bad weather, a build-up occurs. Once the wind changes direction, possibly a hundred species of birds will move at once, their vast numbers creating a wave.

Steady southerly winds in the latter half of April gave the migration clockwork regularity and on time, on April 20, three of the commonest warblers arrived at the Point—the yellow-rumped or myrtle warbler, the common yellowthroat, and the black-and-white. Hundreds of the three species descended on the park, but they did not compete for food, explaining why they migrate together. I saw the yellow-rumped warblers high in the trees, feeding on tiny insects attracted to the flowering buds and the newly opened leaves. The yellowthroat, nicknamed the "bandito" because the male has a black mask across his face, feeds in low bushes and shrubs, and the black-and-white generally feeds off the boughs, trunks, and branches of trees, like a nuthatch or treecreeper.

The wintering sparrows had left now, but their niche was filled briefly by the arrival of other sparrows, like the finely marked field sparrow I found one morning. The field sparrow scampered up a grassy bank overlooking the boating lake, and a little later the trilling call of the yellow warbler, another new arrival, rose from a willow overhanging the water. The bird, a male with maroon brush strokes on its chest, flew out into the open to hawk an insect and returned to the willow to continue singing.

•   •   •

The sun shone strong and hard on April 24, and it was not a time to die. Half the leaves were out and white and pink flowers, hanging in tassels or lifting upward in cones, festooned the park. As he cycled to work Michael Anthony Bradley would have heard the song of the yellow warbler, the harsh notes of the busy blue jay, and he would have smelled the scent of the flowering white cherry. A family out for their first picnic of the year found the body of the 35-year-old Bradley sprawled over his bicycle near 108th Street by Harlem Meer, a lake in the northeast corner of the park. He had been shot once in the left eye and, after the police were called, Bradley was pronounced dead at the scene. Bradley worked as a doorman at an apartment block on the Upper East Side; he had been cycling to work from his home in the Bronx. He did not always go via Central Park, but neighbors said on sunny, pleasant days he preferred to take that route.

Michael Bradley, born in Ireland and recently a naturalized American, would be the first of ten people to die violently in the park during the year.

It was not a requiem for the Irish doorman who, on pleasant days, cycled through the park, but it might have been. That evening a woman in a maroon smock, which failed to conceal her heavy pregnancy, sat on a rocky outcrop near East Seventy-ninth Street, playing a flute.

•   •   •

Half an hour after seeing a male robin tugging at a kite string on the Great Lawn, I saw another dangling from an oak, nylon fishing line tangled around one of his feet. Several times the robin managed to flutter to the branch above him but the line, also wrapped around the branch, merely pulled him down in a flurry of beating wings. All the time the line was getting tighter, but he was high in the tree, and I could not reach him. While the robin struggled to free himself, his mate sat in a nearby branch, twittering softly, unable to comprehend what was happening.

A day later the robin was dead, his body with outstretched wings swinging in the breeze. His female hopped through the woods in search of another male. There was no time to lose for the female. The nesting season was short; she had to be wooed, build a nest and raise two or even three broods in just a few months.

In their haste to build nests, the robins and blue jays had not waited for leaf buds to pop, for trees to become impenetrable jungles of foliage. The nest structures, which were often built low in trees and shrubs, now stood out bulkily, a sure target for vandals. The warblers—which do not nest in the park—would have to wait before starting the mating and nesting ritual. Males were moving through to establish territories, soon to be followed by the females. One bird species that did not have to worry about defending a nesting territory or building a nest was the brown-headed cowbird. In a black cherry in the Ramble a pair of cowbirds sat close together on a twig-branch, like lovebirds in a pet shop. The female crossed to another branch, and the male pursued her, squatted down a few feet away and edged closer until both birds were pressed together. The cowbirds, members of the blackbird and oriole family, are parasitic nesters, the female laying eggs in the nest of warblers and other small birds. The unsuspecting hosts hatch the cowbird egg and do not question why other eggs or young are thrown out of the nest. The chick grows to be larger than the foster parents, and the sight of warblers frantically coming back and forth to feed the greedy chick is one of the sadder sights in nature. Before the European settler came to America, the cowbirds followed bison across the great prairies, relying on them to kick up insects. Even before the buffalos were wiped out, cowbirds started associating with the cattle that replaced them.

Thoughts of buffalos, spreading like brown waves across the prairies, were with me when I passed the Indian Cave looking for more warblers. Something else caught my attention, a mammal; but it was getting dark, and I could not make out its shape. Was it a woodchuck I had seen, sliding across a rock with belly pressed close to the ground to avoid detection? In Central Park?

·   ·   ·

"My schedule will improve as the fever of migration heats my brain." Lambert was keeping in touch by letter again, because I had not seen him for a few weeks. "It never fails to happen. May madness is almost on us and there is no cure. . . ."

· *May* ·

May Day brought a northern waterthrush to the Indian
Cave and a "Rock Against Racism" concert to the Bandshell,
a structure with stage and high domed roof which domi-
nates the only straight path in the park, the conspicuously
formal Mall. It was one of many musical happenings and the
scenario was much the same: a thin blue line of policemen
to keep order, the circling drug dealers selling marijuana
and cocaine, and a park drunk dancing to the music with his
trousers sagging around his backside. The amplified music
could be heard from the Point, where a large, brown bat
flew over my head, its large ears and canvas wings veiny in
the daylight. The bat appeared to collide with a tree. I went
to investigate and found the bat had merely landed flat
against the bark, and was panting. Then it was off again, on
the next leg of its migration. I later established the bat was,
in fact, officially called a big brown bat, and it would be
followed a little later by a smaller cousin, the red bat.

The area that is now Central Park had a mammal population as diverse as anything found in the eastern United
States before the European settlement of Manhattan. Only
ten indigenous species of mammals have managed to remain there consistently, these being five species of bats, the
grey squirrel, cottontail rabbit, eastern mole, short-tailed

shrew, and the chipmunk (the rats and house mice found in the park are of a species introduced to the United States from Europe).

The chipmunk, which I was told inhabited the woodland bordering the Fifty-ninth Street Pond, eluded me all year, and the raccoon threatened to do likewise. Raccoons are common on the green fringes of New York City, but their appearance in Central Park is generally believed to be an act of man. They have been forsaken as pets, and usually they have no fear of humans. A raccoon had been seen curled up, asleep, in a tree near the boathouse in the last week of April. I studied the tree for an entire afternoon but could not pick out the animal. This experience raised the possibility that another mammal, the woodchuck, could survive in the park without detection—if one had been released there. I was convinced I had sighted a woodchuck in the Indian Cave at the end of April, and I returned to the same location a few days later, at dawn when the grass was still wet with dew, and the first catbird of the year mewed at me from a low branch. I did not have to look far for the woodchuck, because it was staring at me from the entrance to the cave. The size of the woodchuck surprised me; it was larger than I had expected. When it established I was not a threat, it moved out of its hiding place to feed. The hairs on its stout body had a frosted appearance, and it slid across the grass to nibble at fresh shoots. If it had been someone's pet, it seemed the height of cruelty to release the woodchuck in the park where it would not find a woodchuck community, and a mate. The poor animal, like a migrating bird stranded in a foreign land, was destined to spend the rest of its life in solitude. It would survive until schoolboy vandals, hunting with rocks, caught up with it; or it would be killed by poison put down by the Parks Department to control rats.

Gangs of schoolboys roaming the park posed a danger

not only to the animals and birds. Some of the mugging of park users is attributed to high school students, especially the robbing of other children, and in April a birder had been threatened with a baseball bat after he refused to take the picture of a gang of youths (he had taken his camera into the park to photograph woodcocks). During May I had my own brush with vandals when I found myself surrounded by a gang armed with stones and sticks. Selfishly, I was relieved to discover they were pursuing squirrels and not me. The youths had cornered a squirrel against a boulder, but the squirrel escaped and climbed a pine, dodging behind the trunk as the rocks were hurled at it. I shouted in protest but, counting about fifteen boys, between thirteen and sixteen years of age, all bending to pick up a fresh supply of ammunition, I backed off.

To be intimidated by schoolchildren is an affront to an adult's dignity, especially when the adult stands six feet three inches tall, weighs 180 pounds and, in years gone by, has confronted risk and danger in pursuit of an outdoor experience. But the mountains, deserts and seas, and the creatures that inhabit them, mean no real harm to those who accept them on their conditions. I felt a different kind of fear in the park, a dry-mouthed apprehension, and, after the incident involving the vandals, for a few weeks I adopted the same strategy as an old couple I often found at the boathouse in the mornings. They delayed over a cup of coffee to await an escort of other birders.

The mugging threat was particularly annoying in the spring because it cut off areas where rare birds might be located. Even the sighting by an intrepid birder of a prothonotary warbler—one of the rarest warblers to come through in the spring—failed to entice any other birders to the location, the Pool at West 100th Street. Because the top section of the park borders some of the meanest streets of the city, birders generally consider it "out of bounds."

•   •   •

A popular out-of-town birding trip during the spring is a weekend journey to the Delmarva Peninsula, where birds rare in the park are easier to see. Prothonotary warblers are common in a swamp in Whaleysville, Maryland, and another rare bird for the park, the yellow-throated warbler, is found in nearby Mitford State Park. I joined one of those trips in May with a group of other park birders. We drove over a thousand miles in three days. The sight of the warblers was worth it, but we could have stayed at home. The two species were spotted in Central Park during the same weekend and I missed them for my park list.

The first week of May had brought westerly and north-westerly winds, raising hopes of a wave day when the wind finally changed direction to the south. A busy workday kept me in the canyons of the city all day on May 7, but an uncanny feeling told me I should really be in the park. I did not have time to listen to a weather report to determine which way the wind was blowing, but every time I looked skyward blue jays were strung out across the sky, hundreds of them, in undulating flight from the south.

Lunch-hour in Times Square—above the traffic drone and the honking of horns came the sound of a man drawing attention to a topless bar: "Lovely dames, no cover, check 'em out." And high above the lovely ladies with no cover and their hustler came the call of the laughing gull. In the novelty shops on Times Square it is possible to buy a little plastic laughing man who, when you pull a cord, makes the same maniacal, boisterous sound of the gulls. I thought the gulls were laughing at me, caught amid all those people, the porn cinemas, the bag ladies, junkies, prostitutes, pimps, and the smell of urine rising from the entrances of the Times Square subway station.

Passing the United Nations building a little later I saw

the flags of the UN's 157 member states fluttering madly to the north side of their poles, indicating a southerly wind. It was time to call a halt to my business day and head for the park. I jumped on a subway train at Grand Central and counted the stops—Fifty-first, Fifty-ninth, Sixty-eighth and freedom from the crushed and stale-air underworld at Seventy-seventh.

Immediately upon entering the park, it was obvious it was a wave day. Bird song was everywhere and in twenty paces I picked up two new species for the year; another ground-feeding warbler, an ovenbird, and a Swainson's thrush. My list for the year had stood at eighty-eight species, and in the next hour I would see eleven more. One of the birders who had been in the park since early morning counted ninety species; and when a group of bird watchers compared notes at the end of the day, they determined there were at least one hundred different kinds of birds. Ovenbirds and five species of thrushes littered the Ramble, and northern waterthrushes left their favored wet feeding areas for the woods; there was simply no room for them at the crowded lake margins. In all, thirty species of warblers were counted during the day but the highlight for me was a large and dramatic finch, the rose-breasted grosbeak, in a willow overlooking an area of shallow water tucked between the Point and the Ramble, which is known as the Point Lobe.

The wave was over in twenty-four hours but there was still plenty to see. The action had switched from the Ramble to the Turkey oaks at the reservoir. The oaks were in flower, attracting insects, which in turn drew the warblers. And where there was a concentration of small birds I was sure to find a kestrel. On a high poplar, towering above the oaks, I saw one of the predators before it dropped on half-folded wings to close the day on a warbler.

Flickers had started to excavate nesting holes in the dead

limbs of trees when Lambert and Sarah marshaled the birders for the second walk of the year. Sarah, now wearing a white headscarf wrapped in the form of a turban, had all the magnetism of a snake charmer when she went through her dance routine. A mesmerized cyclist passing on the east side circular road ran into the curb and fell off his machine. One of the birders gave the cyclist a tissue to wipe blood from his knee as Sarah, a former schoolteacher, shouted to Lambert: "OK, move 'em out." The snake of birders only moved ten yards, however. Lambert had seen a variety of birds coming to drink at a spring near the car park, and for the next half hour the birders lined the car park fence to observe a blue jay, a purple finch, three species of warblers, and a robin take a bath.

"What's that black and white warbler?" said a newcomer to birding who was learning fast. "Oh, that's a black-and-white warbler," said Lambert by way of explanation.

·   ·   ·

I had passed my first target of one hundred birds and now had to concentrate on seeing some rarities if I were to finally reach one hundred and fifty. Before the bird walk had started, Lambert said a rare Kentucky warbler had been seen in previous days in low bushes on the west side of the park, and I left the bird tour to hunt for it. A bird will often remain in one location for a few days if there is a good food supply, and I soon found the Kentucky warbler—the only one seen in the park that spring—hopping in a bed of daffodils. My good fortune continued the next day when I came across the most interesting and spectacular bird I would see all year. Chasing a calling Northern oriole through a clump of flowering chestnut trees, I gave up when the bird moved into another area of the park. In unfamiliar territory, I headed for the nearest path to regain my bearings and spotted what I thought was the biggest bumblebee I had ever seen. But the "bee" had a needle bill, which it stuck into the flowers of a red maple, and I soon realized I was looking at a ruby-throated hummingbird. The tiny bird, about the size of a matchbox, hovered and then swung in an arc as he fed. The beat of his wings, moving at fifty-five flaps a second, were too fast for the human eye to record. The fragile wings had brought the bird from Mexico, or even farther. He had flown across the Gulf of Mexico and still had hundreds of miles to travel to Massachusetts, New Hampshire, or eastern Canada.

On the gently rising slope above the boathouse car park a bitter fight was taking place that would determine whether a brood of flickers was raised in the park during the summer. The flicker that I had seen calling for a mate in April had now found one, and they were busily enlarging a hollow stump half-way up a beech tree. Every other flicker's nest I had found had been seized by starlings; this pair was determined to reverse this situation. The male clung to the outside of the limb, chipping and prising away pieces of rotten wood from a crack, which led to the hollow area inside. He then clambered inside to continue the carpentry; every few minutes his beak would emerge at the hole to release a shower of wood chippings. He was nervous and reluctant to leave the cavity until the female returned from feeding sorties, to take his place. On one occasion, with the female working inside the hole, the male left the nest site for about an hour, and the female frequently came to the entrance of the hole to look for him. She appeared eager to feed again, but she would not leave the hole. The next day I found the female shrieking in agitation. Gripping the trunk, she lunged wildly at something in the hole, before climbing in herself. Out flew a starling, pursued by the enraged female. Composure restored and ruffled feathers smoothed with preening, the female returned to work.

On the other side of the park a pair of flickers was not so lucky. They had already been dispossessed of their nest-hole and the female fought a last-ditch stand to win it back. The female attacked a starling in the uppermost branches of a birch, and the two birds locked together in combat. So intense was the fight that the flicker and starling fell fifty feet, the golden color of the flicker's underwings blurring with the starling's dark blue plumage. The interlocked birds hit a branch and then thudded against the ground. The flicker splayed out her wings, and I thought she was injured; but she continued to attack the starling in the tall grass before they broke apart, flew back into the tree and started the fight again. The male flicker, making a variety of croaking and chirping sounds, egged on his mate and then dive-bombed another starling, pecking at the back of its head. Four times the female flicker and starling crashed to the ground, but it was the flicker who was sustaining injury, blood matted in her feathers. It appeared the flicker's long bill, although good for drilling trees, was not capable of dealing a deadly blow. The starling was far more agile and, with compact beak, he wounded the flicker when he chose to strike back.

An unwritten law in bird watching forbids the birder to interfere with the course of nature. Birders are supposed to be impartial observers, but I was unabashedly biased toward the flickers. A small rock was close at hand, and I hurled it at the starling, missing the bird. Without remorse, I did this a few times but only succeeded in giving the flicker a scare with a misplaced shot. Now the starling went on the offensive against the flicker, and I reached for another rock. As I bent down, I caught sight of an elderly couple out for a stroll. "Shame on you," said the man taking his wife by the arm. "I'm going to call a ranger."

•   •   •

The vagrant with a sleeping bag, two grips, and an intimate

knowledge of the worst economic crisis since the Great Depression passed me and nodded, without a smile. I felt guilty
about our initial encounter, when I had refused to give him
a quarter. I plunged my hand into my pocket, but the vagrant hurried on. He was tall and thin, with angular features
and hair that was long but well-groomed. Despite the vagrant's outdoor existence, his clothes—brown corduroy
jeans and a knee-length, checked woolen jacket—looked
neat and tidy. I had seen the vagrant four or five times but
this was only the second time we had come face to face.
Walking purposefully, he had always managed to avoid me,
but he approached other park users to panhandle a dime
or quarter from anyone who looked as though they could
afford it.

·   ·   ·

For a month I had been taking food for Billy, leaving it first
near the wall of the police stationhouse and then hiding it
under an outcrop of rock in the Ramble, where Billy had
taken up residence. Billy was shy and elusive but he grew
to know who was leaving the food. Some days I even suspected he was watching out for me, but he gave nothing
away. In all probability, Billy had been dumped as a kitten
—like the turtles who outlived their usefulness as pets—and
I also believed he had been ill-treated, because he was wary
of humans and would usually bolt when people approached.
Now he resisted the urge to run when he saw me, but he
would not let me come too close. The weather had been hot
during the first two weeks of May, and Billy would seek out
the coolness of the shaded glades in the Ramble which,
during the mid-afternoon, were dappled with yellow sunlight.
    The blustery winds of early spring had passed and soft,
May breezes rustled the young, rich leaves. There was not
much water about for the birds; they sought sheltered bath-

ing places in wet areas. The best location to observe warblers and other small birds at close range was a little stream feeding the Point Lobe. A spring emerged from inside a rock crevice and trickled under an overhanging hawthorn, whose roots raised the soil and created pools. The hawthorn also provided cover from surprise attack by a kestrel. One afternoon thirteen species came to drink and bathe in the space of thirty minutes. The smallest birds held back in the hawthorn and a clump of knotweed, patiently waiting for the jays and robins to finish. Everything was orderly until three grackles swept in. One plunged straight into the water and startled the jays into flight, and the others approached the series of pools from different ends, chasing off the warblers waiting in line to take a dip.

The starlings had not been content to oust the flickers from the decaying birch on the west side of the park where I had seen the fight. The tree was also home to a pair of downy woodpeckers, and another pair of starlings had dispossessed them. The downies wanted everyone in the park to know what had happened because they called loudly and, learning from the flickers' battle, employed a different strategy for war. Aware that they could easily be killed by the much larger starlings, the downy woodpeckers avoided direct contact and engaged in hit-and-run attacks. Finally they were forced into retreat and the downies, North America's smallest woodpeckers, started hunting for another hole—this time too small for a starling to squeeze through.

The migration had now peaked and so had the controversy over the cutting of trees. Parks staff doing the lumbering were being booed in the Ramble, the petition against cutting was presented to the Central Park administration, and *The New York Times* ran a front page article on the conflict. But the trees continued to come down. It was all a question of priorities, said park administrator Elizabeth Barlow in a letter to *The New York Times*. Either you retain dying and dead trees for the birds or you weed them out and create a neatly manicured park like the one envisaged by Olmsted and Vaux.

The Parks Department had not forgotten the birds altogether. More than two thousand berry-bearing plants, which attract birds, had been planted, mainly on the Point. I disagreed with the cutting program; yet I had to concede the shrubs had attracted birds. The Point had proven my best bird watching location in April and May, and it was from there on the afternoon of May 11 that I saw two birds of prey, one of them a new species. High in the sky, watching below them with side-to-side motions of the head, the two large hawks circled in thermals. The bigger of the birds was a red-tailed hawk and moving northward with it was a broad-wing. I headed north myself hoping for another look at the raptors, but I only reached a disused children's paddling pool near the Pinetum. Surrounded by elms, the pool, which forms a dusty bowl in summer, was now flooded by a couple of inches of muddy water, making it an ideal haunt for migrating shore birds. A solitary sandpiper waded amid the thick mud and half bricks and beer cans. The slender bird, on stilt legs, daintily picked its way through the trash, probing for grubs. The solitary sandpiper is a loner as its name suggests and is mainly found on small ponds or on mud flats. Next day the slate-gray bird, with a white eye-ring that resembles a ship's porthole, was still at the paddling pool and had been joined by a rarity for the park, a least sandpiper. The second shore bird was only the size of a sparrow and scurried about the pond in a completely different manner from its bigger cousin—fast and erratic and lacking the latter's poise and elegance. The arrival of the two sandpipers meant a third member of the family, a spotted sandpiper, was probably in the park, and I went in search of it, not wanting to risk missing the bird in the spring. I could not find it at all the regular shore bird locations, like the Fifty-ninth Street Pond or the boating lake. The last place to check was the Pool at West 100th Street, where the prothonotary warbler had been discovered earlier in the month. Frequently I was informed that the top end of the park was unsafe at any time and, failing to find any of the birders keen to walk the couple of miles from the Ramble to 100th Street, I went by myself. It was late morning, there were quite a few people out, and I stuck to the west circular drive. A group of black schoolkids was being given a biology lesson on the grassy banks of the Pool. Some had nets and were hauling out bullfrog's spawn to take back to class, where they would watch the tadpoles hatch. A boy fell in and the teacher screamed, and the boy, crying, scrambled out of the water. The teacher held him up—a bedraggled example of what happens to kids who don't watch what they are doing. I anticipated finding a spotted sandpiper at the Pool, but I did not expect it to be wading among the kids, unafraid of their noise. The bird's plain white chest and belly was now gaining its spotted breeding plumage. The sandpiper was like a wind-up toy, bobbing and teetering. When it finally grew nervous of the schoolkids, it refused to fly, preferring instead to run into the undergrowth surrounding the pond in its hunt for insects.

•   •   •

A printed line on a poster that said "Adults must be accompanied by a child" had been crossed out by someone having second thoughts about banning the grown-ups. But not many adults were in the Delacorte Theater for what was termed a protest concert to draw attention to the horrors of nuclear war. A movement of eight to eighteen-year-olds calling itself "Future generations for nuclear disarmament" had arranged a program of poetry and music, but the adults missing this protest would have their day during the next month when what was believed to be the largest anti-nuclear rally ever recorded, anywhere, would cover the Great Lawn.

A solitary sandpiper came to the Belvedere Lake, which nudges the back of the theater's stage, while the children were applauding a poem called "Survival." The sandpiper had survival in mind, too, but the word had a connotation that predated the brief history of nuclear weapons, or that occupation, peculiar to *Homo sapiens,* called war.

·　　　·　　　·

My checklist of birds had gone better than I had expected. I had now seen all the common or regular warblers, except one, the Blackburnian, which most birders regard as the prettiest of the family. So sorties for the Blackburnian—the twenty-eighth warbler I would see that year—started, with my first call being the Turkey oaks by the reservoir. It was on one of these hunts that I first saw a vagrant, whom birders call "the sweeper." For reasons trapped in a tangled, confused mind, the vagrant had an obsession with keeping Central Park clean, and when I came across him he was holding a giant broom of the type city-employed sweepers use. He was sitting on a bench, gazing up at the Turkey oaks through sunglasses and matted, long hair that fell over his face. He was about thirty, but had the appearance of a man in his sixties. Every few minutes "the sweeper" jumped to his feet to start sweeping furiously, pushing the litter and leaves into neat piles. He merely left the piles where they were before moving on to another bench. And on days when I did not see the sweeper, I would find evidence of his sweeping over large areas of the park.

The Blackburnian warbler is named after an English biologist, Anna Blackburne, who studied specimens of American birds sent to Britain by her brother from New

York State, New Jersey, and Connecticut in the late 1700's. I saw my first Blackburnian in a flowering black cherry in the Ramble on May 16. It was a male in superb summer plumage, bright orange head and chest, coloring he would lose before heading south again in three months' time.

Research into the winter habits of warblers has revealed that many of them assume completely different feeding and territorial characteristics in the months they spend in Central and South America. Some fiercely independent species join mixed flocks of other warblers, possibly explaining why brightly colored birds moult into dull coloration, which makes them less conspicuous in the flock and more acceptable to the other species. The Blackburnian in May plumage stood out a mile; his orange breast had a luminous quality, and a female would not fail to notice him in the thickest of foliage.

Into the third week of May the temperature rose to the eighties, and a female robin gathered a beakful of worms from the bridle path at the reservoir. I followed her to her nest in the fork of a maple and saw my first young birds of the spring. The ugly, bald chicks still had a pink membrane over their eyes, and when the mother arrived four wide-open yellow beaks thrust skyward in unison. Near the Point, a female Northern oriole had nearly completed a pendulous nest of dried grass after six days of hard work. The nest was strung between two thin branches of a London plane, and it swung crazily as a thunderstorm gathered.

A cluster of solemn and disappointed birders gathered in a drizzle, under the umbrella of a tulip tree, on May 22. They nodded in agreement. It looked like the migration was just about over. They had failed to find a warbler that morning—not even the yellow-rumped warbler, which had been common for more than a month—but there was some consolation later in the day when a summer tanager settled in a sourgum. The oriole's nest near the Point now held the female incubating her clutch of three or four eggs and every few minutes the male, resplendent with black head and orange body, arrived to cling to the nest's side and feed his mate through its oval opening. It was one of three oriole nests I had found.

The frenzy of migration had now given way to the rush to feed young. Beaks sprouted from most open nests and adult birds divided the long daylight hours between feeding their young, feeding themselves and defending their nests against predators. Raiding squirrels looked for eggs to smash so they could eat the yolks, and one of the most ferocious battles I saw during the summer involved a pair of blue jays and two nest-raiding squirrels. While a jay sat incubating eggs in her nest atop a maple, the squirrels slowly edged along the branch, flat on their bellies, trying to hide among the leaves. The jay flicked her tail nervously, aware of impending attack. Then she let out a scream, rose from the nest and flew into one of the rodents, pecking it. The dismayed squirrel slipped from the branch but managed to cling with sharp claws to its underside. The male jay, responding to the female's alarm call, swooped in and gave the second squirrel a sharp nip as he passed at great speed. The male repeated his swoops, smacking the large, palmate leaves in which the squirrels were trying to bury themselves. The battle in the treetop brought in other birds as spectators. A curious grackle arrived on the same branch and was unfortunate enough to receive a smack from the male jay. The fight lasted fifteen minutes, the female never straying too far from the nest and both birds pausing for breath, with beaks open, before lunging at the squirrels again. At one point a third blue jay arrived; he planted himself in a branch directly above the nest, to provide extra cover in case a squirrel tried to advance from that direction.

A mockingbird I had seen with three fledglings out of the nest during the previous week now had only two, when I found her again during the Memorial Day weekend, the unofficial start of summer. I assumed the third chick was killed by a predator, and I hoped it was not a human. The kestrel, or even Billy, would have been preferable. The remaining chicks were now well past their early days of vulnerability when they first leave the nest, and they could fly up to ten yards, allowing them to make a rapid, if erratic, escape. From the size of the young I determined the parents had started incubating eggs in mid-April, early for mockingbirds, and already the birds had completed a second nest, to raise another brood. The overworked male soon found himself feeding the young, feeding his female on the nest and, when he had time, finding food for himself. He had a ragged look about him as he hunted insects, grubs and fresh shoots near the south end of the Mall, where the second nest was located in a low bush. Mockingbirds defending territory and young show a belligerence that is fiercer than in any other bird their size, and the male mockingbird, which I had in my sights, policed an area of about twenty square yards, swooping at unsuspecting squirrels, dogs, cyclists, joggers, and vagrants who invaded his patch.

·   ·   ·

A toddler sat in a stroller, raindrops of tears welling in his eyes. His head bowed, the tears ran quickly down the rounded descent of his face. The toddler's father, a youngish man in his early thirties, with an Oxford cloth shirt buttoned to the top and his parted hair unparted in head-thrashing anger, squatted in front of the stroller, pointing a finger at the child. "Now look," he said, his voice rising. "I'm under a lot of pressure. I don't need all this crap."

·   ·   ·

The coming of summer also brought the bird most associated with the season—the barn swallow—in large numbers to the park. The swallows had paused on their migration to hawk insects over the Turkey oaks at the bridle path. The birds, coming from as far away as Argentina, joined a flight of chimney swifts flying low, in wide circles, which took them out over the reservoir. The swallows were arrow silhouettes against the sun but, when I focused binoculars on them, I saw they mixed metallic-blue, red, and cinnamon in their plumage. Occasionally, one of the swallows splayed its wings, spread its forked tail, and took a sip of water on the wing.

Cedar waxwings also arrived on the last day of May to feed in flowering trees on Cherry Hill, a rounded, grassy knoll south of the boating lake. Although the silky, grey-green birds, with red tips to the wings, are sometimes seen in the park in winter, they usually arrive as the last migrants. Their primary food is fruit, and they prefer to rear young when the trees are thick with berries in late summer. The cedar waxwings pushed my bird count to 122 species at the end of May. Collectively, the park's birders had listed 150 species in the bird register—at a cost of two birders mugged.

·   ·   ·

The birders claimed victory. The Parks Department decided not to attack moths with a chemical spray. Instead, a biological agent, a bacterium that attacks only gypsy moth caterpillars, was being used and this, said the department, would prove nontoxic to humans and other wildlife.

In my mailbox was a letter from Lambert, the letter bearing a crayon and ink drawing of Roman gladiators carrying off one of their dead. The corpse bore a striking resemblance to the parks commissioner.

"The armies defeated, the city abandoned," said a hastily scribbled caption under the illustration.

· *June* ·

A green heron stood, statuesque, at the muddy edge of the Fifty-ninth Street Pond. Patiently it waited for ten minutes for a fish or a bullfrog or a tadpole to swim by, its dagger-beaked head bowed. Without luck at this fishing spot, the heron moved to another; it was difficult to detect that the bird was in motion. Slowly, the heron leaned forward to maintain a steady balance as it gradually lifted a long leg and placed it forward. It took the heron all of seven minutes to travel four feet before it froze again, ropey neck compacted into hunched shoulders. A big bullfrog, as long as the heron's beak, paddled by with slow kicks of hind legs, the frog changing direction to avoid what it thought were two stalks jutting from the water. These were the heron's legs and, with a whiplash, the S-shaped neck unfurled so fast I did not see it unfurl at all. The bird swayed and rocked as the stout bullfrog was hauled clear of the water, the amphibian kicking its hind legs and clawing at the air in a swimming stroke. The heron wrestled with the bullfrog for several minutes, smashing it against a piece of broken brick to stun and kill it. The heron loosened its grip, and turned the bullfrog around with rapid flicks of the beak, so the amphibian's head faced the heron's gape. An exaggerated swallowing gesture, and the bullfrog became a round shape in the heron's throat.

It was June and well into the green heron's breeding season. I thought the heron might have a mate in the seclusion of a fenced-in forested area behind the Pond, but I was not to see a green heron again for the rest of the summer.

The quest to find new species of birds had now turned into an operation to establish which species were breeding. The ubiquitous European house sparrows—another imported bird from Britain—had made homes in just about every street light casing overhanging the park's circular drive. Grass and long strands of straw stuck out of the light fittings and from the top of one lamppost a piece of transparent plastic trailed in the wind. It was hot in the nests at night, but the large numbers of young sparrows seen in the park by the end of May had proven the lampposts had been a good choice of nesting site. There was also a colony of sparrows nesting at the Delacorte Theater, with scraggy nests built betwen the theater's outer wall and the metal letters spelling its name.

Although most of the chickadees and tufted titmice had moved north of New York City to breed, I discovered two chickadees nesting in a hollow limb near the Point. A rotten branch rising vertically had snapped off; it pointed skyward like a pipe, with just enough of an aperture for the chickadees to build their moss and feather-lined nest cup. I had heard of a pair of titmice raising a family in a snapped-off lamppost during the previous year. This breeding season, however, the pole remained uninhabited. But there was evidence of titmice nesting in other places, and I saw the occasional titmouse carrying food for young in the area of the Azalea Pond, in the Ramble.

A family of cardinals had also set up home in thick shrubbery near the Azalea Pond. I could not find the nest but in the first week of June three young cardinals, two showing the red that would blossom into male plumage, gathered noisily on a branch waiting for mother and father to arrive with food. The birds still had wide yellow beaks, out of proportion with their heads, which gave them a Donald Duck appearance. The fledglings started up a continuous chatter when one of their parents came into sight, and the adult bird went from one to another forcing mushed berries and seeds into their mouths. Three weeks later I saw one of the young males, virtually in full plumage, strutting confidently about the undergrowth of the Ramble. In just about a month a new generation of cardinals had emerged, to continue to grace Central Park with their friendship and beauty.

On the second day of June I checked out the three orioles' nests I knew of—one at the base of the Point, another slung from a black cherry on Cherry Hill, and the third hanging from the low branch of a London plane at the lower, west side lobe of the boating lake. From each nest came the excited chatter of fledglings when they thought their parents were near, the nests bulging with movement like a sack containing kittens. Even a breeze rustling the thick leaves of the planes was enough to set the birds off in their noisy anticipation of receiving a mouthful of food.

A week later the nest at the lake's lower lobe, which was hanging only about ten feet from the ground, had a large stick wedged through it, a stick which had been thrown with some force. The male and female orioles had deserted the nest and it was silent. Only flies moved in and out of the oval opening, and maggots would be eating the carcasses of the baby orioles.

At the reservoir there was an example of another kind of heartlessness. Totally lost and confused, a baby duck with downy brown feathers swam in circles near the south pumphouse, foraging for food among the debris floating in the water. The duckling had traces of a head and neck pattern and at first I thought a pair of ruddy ducks had reared young on the reservoir. A male ruddy duck, in his chestnut summer plumage with white patches on his cheeks, had lingered on the reservoir until late May. But I had not seen a female, and I wondered how it could be possible for ducks to breed on the reservoir without being noticed.

I next saw the duckling resting on the dam wall. Its wing feathers had not yet formed and, without evidence of parents, it appeared the bird had been placed on the reservoir, or thrown over its high fence, from outside. When I told Lambert about the duckling he had a theory: someone out in the country, on a day trip possibly, had come across the duckling, adopted it as a pet and then had second thoughts about it. I saw the duckling one more time, on June 4, and it appeared to be too young to fend for itself. It was starving and certain to die.

·   ·   ·

Seen from one of the jets that wind their way in and out of La Guardia Airport, Central Park is log-shaped, greasy and mossy, the paths and roadways like contours of peeling bark. I was leaving New York on a weekend business trip but my thoughts were with the log. From ten thousand feet I wanted to kick it over, to explore what was underneath. Lambert was down there somewhere, in the Ramble in his yellow bush hat, ignoring the male prostitutes soliciting at the Azalea Pond; he would be looking for nests, or for the caterpillar of the tiger swallowtail butterfly.

An old, decomposing log is the first key to understanding the complexity of the forest. The underside of the log is a microcosm of forest life, hiding salamanders, snakes, insects, and worms; creatures not living in harmony, because some prey on others, but living symbiotically—interrelated and interwoven in the chemistry of the woods.

The city is the human forest; its parks are its logs. And in Central Park it is possible to scrutinize New Yorkers shed of their protective apartment-block shells. But timing is important if you wish to study the park's social balance, and a visit at the wrong time can provide a completely different, and erroneous perspective. The wrong time is any weekend between mid-June and mid-September, because a vital constituent, the city's wealthy, deserts New York on summer weekends and forsakes Central Park. Notices pinned to trees from late May announce that beach homes on Long Island are for rent on a communal basis: "tennis players, joggers and nonsmokers." The notices imply an exclusivity for the young and fit and relatively affluent.

New York's poor get left behind in summer, and Central Park, along with apartment-block rooftops, fire escapes, and front steps, provides relief from a city which is a melting honeycomb of fetid heat.

·   ·   ·

If Central Park belongs to the poor in summer, it also belongs to one ethnic group, the Puerto Ricans, the people and their offspring who have brought their toil and gaiety to the city in the last thirty years, moving into a working class slot vacated by other, older immigrant groups who now summer on Long Island. Because of the Puerto Rican predominance, Spanish is the language of Central Park in summer, and the Latin flavor especially permeates the tunnels of overhanging trees beyond the Ninety-seventh Street transverse, where the park borders Spanish Harlem. On the East and North Meadows extended families spread blankets and collapsible chairs and build fires. The air is full of the aroma of cooking corn and sausage, and children play ball among adults passing half-pints of white rum. Entrepreneurs set up food stalls, scraggy kids with holes in their pants tout iced beer at twenty-five cents over the supermarket price, and the ball fields on each side of the North Meadow seem to be transplanted from San Juan.

Puerto Rican Day is one of the most important events on the park calendar, and a steady rain was not to dampen the occasion for thousands of Puerto Ricans on June 6. The main parade took hours to move along Fifth Avenue; long before it was over many of the spectators had flooded into the park, to gather at the Bandshell along the Mall. Traditionally, the Bethesda Fountain is the focal point for this gathering, but for this year's celebrations an extra contingent of police sealed off its plaza, fearing a graffiti attack and damage to the newly restored fountain. One young Puerto Rican, however, cleared the wooden barricades in one leap, dodged two police officers and then jumped over the wall of the basin that catches the fountain's water. Waving the Puerto Rican flag, the youth climbed the monument's plinth and placed the ensign on a ledge supporting the fountain's winged goddess of water, to wild cheers.

So many people had gathered in front of the Bandshell that the crowd backed up along the Mall, until it encroached on mockingbird territory. The male mocker which, for the past month, had been so determined to defend its patch, moved into an elm, outnumbered. Its two young could fend for themselves, and he was now preoccupied with feeding the second brood of three chicks. At one point two revellers swayed off the Mall and fell onto the muddy grass, shouting and laughing. The mockingbird watched nervously and when they staggered to their feet and moved too close to the nest the angry mocker dove at them. The two men were supporting each other drunkenly; when one saw the mocker, he fell on his face, with his friend tripping over his legs. They lay on the grass, caked in mud, laughing hysterically, and the mockingbird retreated, victorious.

·　　　·　　　·

Heavy rain, and a good time to look for Billy. In bad weather

I knew he would be hiding, snug and warm, in his lair under the outcrop of Manhattan schist. I do not know how the deep crack in the rock had formed, what forces and pressures had caused the rock to fracture at this point, but the fissure created a miniature cave going back about three feet. Billy, being smart, never slept way back in the cave but curled up near its entrance, behind a piece of smooth rock that jutted out on one side. This way he could be out of sight, but in position to run from the cave if danger threatened. I knew Billy was hiding behind a barrier of suspicion, but I was making progress in my efforts to develop a friendship. We now had a fragile, tenuous relationship. I still could not feed him by hand or stroke his shiny black coat but he did not run when he saw me now. If I moved too close, too quickly, he merely backed off, always keeping me in view. I had given him a scare once, by going up to the entrance of his lair without calling his name. He ran past me, snarling, and it took a few weeks of coaxing after that to regain his confidence. I was taking food regularly for him, even though there was plenty of food available in the park, and I always hid these gifts in a fissure a little way above his hiding place, where the rats would not get at it.

I found Billy hiding and called his name slowly, softly. He poked his head around the corner of the cave. I showed him the food, a whole fish this time, and a small container of milk. I left it at the hiding place, but Billy did not come out in the rain. Only mad dogs and Englishmen go out in the Central Park rain. He would wait for it to stop.

•   •   •

Wandering toward the Bow Bridge, which spans the boating lake in a lazy iron sweep, I saw the vagrant, who knows all about unemployment, coming from the other way. He looked up and saw me and wanted to turn back, but it would be obvious he was trying to avoid me. So he kept walking, nodded as we passed, and then swung around to call to me. "Hey, there's this bird I want to tell you about. . . ."

At the south end of the park, bordering the Fifty-ninth Street Pond is a bird sanctuary, enclosed by an eight-foot-high fence. The vagrant said he climbed the fence every night to find a place to sleep: "It's safe in there. No muggers, no crazies. You get a good night's sleep there, peaceful." Then he said that after dark large birds swooped into the sanctuary and dropped to the edge of the Pond. They were big and gray, with long beaks. And when the moon was up, they looked white, like ghosts. But he said the birds did not scare him and on one occasion, when someone else had been in the sanctuary, wandering about, the birds had croaked and alerted him to a prowler. The birds, he said, also had long crests, which he could only see in the moonlight, or when they were silhouetted against the lights of Fifty-ninth Street.

He was describing night herons, and when we met subsequently he would stop and tell me what the herons had been up to.

·　　　　·　　　　·

The female oriole feeding young on the Point came to drink in front of the boathouse as the biggest crowd Central Park had seen in its 125 years was assembling. It was early on the morning of June 12, and police officers in crisp blue shirts and polished silver insignia sipped coffee at the cafeteria tables overlooking the lake. The police were part of a five-thousand-strong contingent, which had been marshaled for what was later described as the largest political protest in United States history. A grackle also came to drink while a police radio crackled out the message that an antinuclear march was moving off from the United Nations headquarters three miles away.

"Let's go," said a police sergeant, and the cafeteria emptied.

On Fifth Avenue, a group of twenty people took up position on the sidewalk, clustered behind a banner announcing they were from the Congress of Senior Citizens of Greater New York. Every available space by the roadside was filling up and a hurrying crowd preceding the march surged by, making its way to the protest venue on the Great Lawn. In this first wave I saw the man in military green who stands alone under an oak on the west side of the park. Away from his oak, the man looked apprehensive, constantly looking back to see if the marchers were gaining on him. What he saw was a swollen river of bobbing heads. As the marchers burst on the senior citizens lining the sidewalk at Seventieth Street there were cheers and handclaps in salute of the aged. An old man, in a yellow baseball cap, gave a clenched fist salute in response, and the rest of the old folk applauded the marchers.

Above Fifth Avenue a crow circled, gazing down in curiosity, and directly under him was a man with a banner reading: "All creatures will be lost in a nuclear holocaust." When the initial wave of marchers had reached Central Park, traveling on two routes via Seventh Avenue on the West Side and Fifth Avenue on the East Side, marchers were still setting out from assembly points near the United Nations. It was like that for hours; long after the speeches and the music had started, people were still pouring into the park. Tucking myself behind a large lady, who was wearing a safari outfit with a pith helmet and mosquito-net veil, I found myself part of the protest. A choir named The Singing Voice of Japan had set up stage in a piece of masonry called the Richard Morris Hunt Memorial at Seventieth Street. Richard Morris Hunt did not look amused, and on a pillar above his marble head a boy of a man, with long fair hair and blue T-shirt, sat crosslegged and motionless in meditation.

Through lines of police, the river of people meandered

onto the Great Lawn and flooded at its sides. Police said a crowd that had swelled to at least five hundred thousand a few hours after the rally started might have reached seven hundred thousand by late afternoon. A park ranger estimated three quarters of a million people and other parks staff suggested, with all the coming and going, there might have been a million people on or near the Great Lawn during the course of the day.

The rally had been organized by a coalition of peace groups and a general theme of the speakers was that the nuclear arms race, while threatening mankind with extinction, was already damaging life on earth. A horrifying vision of what the detonation of a nuclear bomb would do for New York City was offered by Carol Bellamy, President of the City Council, as she stood outside the United Nations welcoming the marchers to New York: "Look around you for just one moment, my friends, at the beauty of New York's urban landscape, then consider that the detonation of a single one-megaton bomb would flatten every building in sight. The flash of white light, the force of the fireball, would within seconds char, batter, and crush every living being within a nine-mile radius, the winds spreading radiation and fire far beyond."

When the march started moving a man held a sign reading "Don't blow it—good planets are hard to find," and a little ahead of him a woman from Vermont carried a crying baby on her back. At one point, when the Vermont contingent paused to let others catch up with them, the woman knelt and started to breast-feed her baby.

"We're thinking of our babies," said a speaker at the Great Lawn. "There are no communist babies; there are no capitalist babies. A baby is a baby is a baby."

On one of the few patches of open grass, to the side of the speaker's platform and the battery of amplifiers, a little girl in Alice-in-Wonderland dress sat with a brown rabbit. On a cardboard square, looped with string around one of her buttons, she carried a message: "I Made History, June 12, 1982."

·   ·   ·

The members of the Central Park Model Yacht Club were not happy. First the antinuclear rally prevented many model boat enthusiasts from attending the two-day annual championships on the Conservatory Pond. And on the second day it rained, forcing the championships to be cut short. But all was not lost. The twelve skippers, who had ignored the consistent downpour to guide their boats around a triangular course marked by orange buoys, were later treated to a home movie of a 1979 model yacht race. The film, accompanied by sunny smiles of approval, was projected onto a makeshift screen leaning on a ladder at the Conservatory boathouse.

The second brood of the South Mall mockingbirds left the nest on June 20. Three fledglings made their way safely across the lawn and up into the low branches of a linden. Meanwhile, the hard-pressed male, dubbed "Papa Mocker" by the bird watching fraternity, started work on a third nest.

In the last week of June the park's first ducklings appeared on the boating lake. A watchful mother mallard led eight tiny balls of fluff across the water, the chicks bobbing like toys in her wake. Later in the day I came across mother and chicks squatting on a low, flat rock near the Indian Cave. I tried to avoid disturbing them, stopping in my tracks and slowly backing off. But mother was nervous. One by one she nudged her chicks into the algae-green water with her bill. Sensing danger, the brood pressed closer to her body and in one feathery mass they headed for deeper water.

·   ·   ·

"I looked for your gashawk, but the planes were too high to

make them out with the naked eye," said Lambert, referring to my plane trip. He would not train binoculars on an aircraft, which was a form of sacrilege. I could understand his jargon, and I finally felt accepted as a cult member. A "gashawk," a play on the name of a bird, a goshawk, is part of a vocabulary of about fifty words birders use to proclaim their identity (you will not find a definition of such words as a "kettle," meaning a spiral of birds of prey, in any dictionary). To be taught the jargon of a community, by one of that community's members, means you have passed all the tests leading to acceptance; you have arrived and, in this case, are a fully fledged Central Park birder whose word and bird sightings will be taken seriously. It is a mark of trust.

Lambert, although he did not know it, had also eased my transition to New York City, allowing me to eventually pass what I term the "BLT test." The city jargon is a vital tool in piercing New York's apparent hostility, which, I believe, basically comes down to a lack of communication.

The BLT test? Try asking for a bacon, lettuce, and tomato sandwich, without mayonnaise, to take away, with an English accent, while being served by someone who only speaks Spanish in a Times Square delicatessen in the frenzy of lunch hour. "BLT, ho' the mayo, to go" made life so much simpler and, with time, I could order other things with confidence. I also learned to ride the subway lines other than the one linking my home with the office, understanding the "BMT," the "IND" and the "IRT" (acronyms you will not find on a subway map), and I mastered the tipping formula in a taxi, so I did not get a trail of abuse in the taxi's slipstream.

Lambert was generous with his knowledge of New York but, like the city itself, much about him remained a secret. I had known him nearly six months and did not know whether he was married, had children, or what he did for a living. He never directed the conversation that way.

•   •   •

Lynn was thirty, a secretary from a small town in Nebraska and described herself as attractive in a Nebraska sort of way. It took all the courage Lynn could muster to step off the sidewalk of Fifth Avenue on June 27 and join the annual Gay Parade. For forty-five minutes she had stood on the curb watching thousands of members of the city's homosexual community troop by in celebration of a 1969 clash between gays and police in Greenwich Village, which is considered to have given birth to the Gay Liberation Movement. There were marching bands, baton twirlers and sidewalk sympathizers with placards reading "Mom and Dad for Gays" and "Grandma for Homosexuals." Lynn had not wanted to join in, telling her girlfriend she was not ready to "come out of the closet" publicly. Then a woman shouted, "I'm for families, not gays," and Lynn pulled her girlfriend off the curb and into the march, which was culminating in a rally on the Great Lawn. The organizers of the Gay and Lesbian Pride March, as it is known, said a hundred thousand people had gathered for the march and rally. Police said forty thousand had taken part.

"We're marching to show our pride and to show ourselves how many of us there are," said one of the leaders of the march. "We like to be visible and let people know we come from all walks of life. We are everywhere."

"Mama Mocker" had been incubating her third clutch of eggs for five days as a group of laughing gays returning from the rally passed the nest site. They were mobbed by her mate, weary now but reconciled to his role of provider and protector for the third time in three months.

•   •   •

"Come," said Lambert, tersely, because he was in a hurry to

complete some unexplained business in town. "I've got something to show you." What he showed me near the Azalea Pond was a house sparrow who, he said, had "gone back to nature." The male sparrow had decided he was a hippie, a dropout, a sparrow who rejected the organized, highly structured society of the sparrow colony, which relies on man for its nesting sites. This rebel sparrow had built a nest in a tree, the structure being an untidy mess of straw and paper laced with string to the outer twigs of a pin oak. Lambert had watched the sparrow building the nest for a week and now, as I arrived, it was virtually completed. The proud sparrow, puffing out his chest, twittered from a twig above the precariously swaying nest, trying to attract a female to come take a look at his home. But not many came. After three days the proud and independent sparrow started to display an element of self-doubt by flying to a nearby disused lamppost to study a "conventional" nest there. From the site of the second nest the unconventional sparrow managed to persuade a female to follow him to his own nest. The method of persuasion included a sharp peck, and the reluctant female followed the male under threat of assault. But even the male's bullying and insistent twittering did not convince her this could be home to her brood of five chicks. After another sharp peck from the male, she even went so far as to inspect the nest's scruffy interior but remained unimpressed. She had been born in a lamppost casing, so were her mother and father, and she wanted it that way for her offspring. To translate her preference into human terms, she wanted a condominium, not a house on the prairie.

The nest remained unoccupied all summer.

The house sparrow, like the starling, was introduced to the United States in the late 1800's, and to say that it has prospered in the New World is an understatement. The sparrow, a member of the weaver-finch family of Africa,

Europe and Asia, is a supreme opportunist, and it has strayed far from what is believed to have been its original home in North Africa. One theory about its widespread distribution holds that it first latched on to man and his settlements in the Nile Delta, when Egyptian civilization was dawning there. When man discovered how to cultivate and store crops successfully, the sparrow soon learned that man had a perennial supply of food, and cultivated him. As civilization spread, and with it man-made structures that provided nesting sites, through the Middle East and into Europe, the sparrow followed. Then it followed Britain's colonial process throughout much of the rest of the world, being taken to early coastal settlements as a reminder of home to the settlers and then spreading wherever the colonialists had set up home.

· *July* ·

A Central Park bench offers the perfect antidote to the
United States' largest city. It was from a bench on the Great
Lawn during 1982 that I surveyed my life, a wandering
existence very much like the winding, rambling paths of the
park. I had been a journalist for my entire working life, some
nineteen years, working on some very good and some very
bad newspapers. In recent years I had traveled to Africa as
a roving correspondent, initially going to South Africa on
what I told myself would be a year-long working holiday. I
had stayed on the continent for nine years. The wildlife of
Africa, its abundance and easy accessibility, persuaded me
to stay every time I had thoughts about moving on. I had
grown blasé about the sight of a pride of lions, or a three-
hundred-strong herd of elephants, and when it was finally
time to leave I thought I was an expert, I knew it all and,
anywhere in the world, I would be something of a wildlife
guru, with all that Africa experience behind me, all those
African tales to tell. A latter-day Kipling.

Many times I held court in the boathouse cafeteria on
subjects that ranged from "what to do if you come across a
hippopotamus out of water" (run) to "the first step in treat-
ing a gaboon viper bite" (amputate). But my knowledge and
understanding of the workings of nature, its complexity and

continental interdependence, was shallow and superficial. Lambert knew a thousand times more than I, although I had visited a thousand more places. I could not compete with a man who had seen more than two hundred species of birds in Central Park or had identified a greater number of butterfly and moth species on Manhattan than are found in the entire British Isles. My Africa stories had finally stopped in the telling when Lambert had read me a quotation from an author I had not heard of before, the late Hal Borland:

> He knows most about the world who knows best that world which is within his own footsteps. Not all hills and valleys are alike, but unless a man knows his own hills and valleys he is not likely to understand those of another. . . .

•   •   •

Six in the morning on the first day of July. A black-crowned night heron has its eye on the chicks of a female mallard. The heron stands hunched at the edge of the reservoir; the mallard is leading her brood of eight down the steep concrete bank to the water. The mallard, the second to rear chicks in the park, has nested in scrub sprouting from the stone embankment. The brood has probably hatched the previous day. They are tiny. One chick lags behind and the heron strikes from a few feet away. The mallard swings around in a cacophony of quacks and startles the heron. This gives the chicks a chance to slide into the water, and the determined red-eyed heron takes to the wing again and swoops at them. The heron plunges its foot into the reservoir for balance but cannot find its grip on the steeply sloping bottom. The chicks, their first time in water, dive and surface close to their mother, who sweeps in tight circles like a naval destroyer searching for a submarine. The mallard family, intact, heads rapidly away from the bank, and the heron is in hunched posture again, waiting for the chicks to return to the bank, waiting for a second chance to strike.

·   ·   ·

A small but enthusiastic band of butterfly enthusiasts met at the boathouse cafeteria sharp at 10 A.M. The group was led by Lambert and another nature-lover called Mervyn, whom I had not met before, introduced himself with a firm hand-shake. With temperatures rising steadily through June to the anticipated eighties throughout July, the butterfly season had arrived and Lambert announced that he had already counted six species on his way to the cafeteria. Interrupting a donut and coffee breakfast, the members of the party solemnly signed their names as witnesses to Central Park's second-ever butterfly count. Then off they went on a walk through the glades, hearts and voices rising at the sight of any erratic flutter through the leaves.

"Mourning cloak," Lambert said authoritatively as the species swept by and settled on a flower. "We've already got that." There were also red admirals, monarchs, alfalfas, spring azures and question marks. And then the sight of the magnificent tiger swallowtail at the flooded and disused children's paddling pool, which had been so good for birds in the early spring. The tiger swallowtail is a large, yellow butterfly with striking black pattern on broad wings that taper to a rounded point beyond the insect's body. This was a perfect specimen, the sunlight making it dazzle like gold tinfoil; the butterfly twisting and turning, fluttering and gliding. A robin sprang from the shade of an elm, displaying the agility of a swallow as it chased the insect. And then a sharp "crack." The robin nailed the swallowtail with its beak and threw it to the ground. The rapid beat of the butterfly's wings died in slow flaps, the robin biting at the body of the insect. "That goddamn bird," said Lambert, pulling his favorite bush hat over his eyes. Mervyn, with creaselines scarring a windburned face, was standing at the disused children's pool remembering his childhood of fifty years ago. His eyes followed a dragonfly, which had dark tips on transparent wings.

"When I was a kid we believed that if a dragonfly landed on you, you would die. So we killed them. We must have been mad," he said quietly.

Someone said that he had seen a dragonfly resting, exhausted, on a wall in Times Square a few days previously.

"What 's a dragonfly doing in Times Square?" someone else asked. The question went unanswered as all eyes now followed the dragonflies, which flew low across the mud, stopping to hover in mid-air.

The butterfly count clocked twenty-six species.

·　　　　　·　　　　　·

The Loula D. Lasker Pool opened in the last week of June after skinny little black kids had gathered at its fence for the preceding two months hoping that someone would let them in. On fine, sunny days the kids were always at the fence and numbers had increased as days grew longer and hotter through June. The pool is the only official swimming pool in the park and the only way the poor kids from the adjoining streets of Harlem can keep cool during the long, hot summer. Into July it grew very hot and sticky and, long after the gates had closed with a clang of steel, the sound of splashing and laughter and delighted shrieks came from the Loula D. Lasker Pool. Up to three thousand people have been known to use the pool illegally at night, gaining access through neat holes in the fence opened up with wirecutters. Sometimes a man would come to fix the fence, but before he had returned to the park's maintenance depot, the kids had it cut open again. There was something unusual about this night, although the shrieking kids might not have noticed it. The bright full moon had its usual summer halo of humidity but during the early hours of the next morning, July 6, the moon began to vanish. At 2 A.M. the shadow of the planet Earth, where the skinny Harlem kids were swimming illegally in the Loula D. Lasker Pool, began to creep across it. By 2:38 A.M. the moon could be seen as a copper dot during the longest total lunar eclipse in 123 years. Out on Fifth Avenue, at the intersection of Fifty-ninth Street, moon-watchers had gathered.

"So what?" said a woman wanting to get back to the Oak Room bar in the Plaza Hotel. "Wait a moment and you'll see the shadow of your nose," said her irritated male companion. "Go f--- yourself," replied the woman, self-consciously fingering a nose larger than most.

·   ·   ·

Billy liked Boston scrod more than he liked jerky, and he liked jerky a lot. I made this discovery one afternoon after I had forgotten to buy jerky and, three blocks from the park, made a hurried purchase of scrod at a fish store on East Eighty-second Street. For some months Billy had been losing his nervousness when I talked to him at the entrance of his cave. And when I first produced the scrod he came forward to within two feet of me, but he would not cross the threshold of actual contact.

·   ·   ·

Six days after its bombardment by the night heron, the mallard family on the reservoir was still intact. With temperatures hitting eighty-four degrees, mother and babies sheltered under a bush of willow on a stretch of dam wall that still had to be cleared of rogue vegetation by maintenance men slowly working their way around the reservoir's circumference during the summer. A chick wandered from the female and started tugging at a reed bent double in the water. Mother scolded the baby with a low whistle; the fledgling scurried back to her side.

Evidence of the vulnerability of the young mammals and birds was everywhere in the park. A flattened robin, speckled with youth, lay on a footpath, and on the circular drive I counted the bodies of six or seven young gray squirrels. The first of two broods of squirrels had appeared early in the spring. The young were virtually identical to the adults, if slightly smaller and thinner, but their stupidity gave them away. The young were unbelievably tame, coming up close and showing a slowness to recognize a threatening gesture. In other creatures wariness is a basic instinct from birth, but this did not seem to be the case with the squirrels. They learned the hard way, and either schoolboys with rocks or cars on the circular drive kept the park's squirrel population in check.

Young birds, though, could also show gross stupidity; perhaps out of confusion, the trauma of being confronted by open spaces after the security of the nest. On the East Side drive, where the road follows the curve of the reservoir, a catbird battled to keep a brood of two chicks together. The fledglings were on the road surface when one became separated from the mother by a stream of marathon runners pounding south. The mass of athletes thickened, and the bird was driven to the other side of the road, the parent trying at first to dive at the runners in a futile attempt to frighten them off. Then she flew to the young catbird, leaving the other fledgling to fend for itself momentarily in the nest-site bush, a hawthorn. After the bulk of runners had passed, she managed to coax her offspring to fly low and fast back across the road.

By mid-July the mallard family on the reservoir was

down to four ducklings from the original eight. It appeared
the night heron had perfected a technique for attacking and
killing the chicks. But the second family of mallards, on the
boating lake, was still doing well. Perhaps to avoid the herons, the mother had marched the brood a quarter of a mile
to the Belvedere Lake. The ducklings, by now the size of
pigeons, still had not grown wing feathers and could not fly.
They were lucky they had not run into Billy on the walk. He
had proven he was not afraid of taking the bigger birds,
because I had seen him with a dead pigeon. And a duckling
would have made a pleasant change from his usual park diet
of house sparrows and starlings.

·   ·   ·

One hundred years ago and more, before apartment air
conditioning, it was common for the poorer people of New
York to drift from their overcrowded tenements to the park,
to sleep there during those frequent, unbearable nights
when summer humidity forms a steamy blanket over the
city. Now only the bag people, without possessions to have
stolen, and the crazies and crooks roam and sleep in the
park's acres by night. It is a pity the park is not accessible
during the summer nights, because it has an uncanny calm
at this time: the thick, hot air cushions the hard sounds of the
streets and the roar of jet aircraft overhead. Around the
reservoir, with water evaporating rapidly, the air hangs still
and heavy and is only pierced by the rhythm of the cicadas
and crickets or an occasional high-pitched squeal from a bat
using echo location to detect insects around the lights on the
reservoir footpath. Dawn comes slowly, imperceptibly; the
trees taking shape as rounded masses of black as the sky
turns from ink-black to navy blue, to opal. Then the sun
bursts above the Fifth Avenue apartment blocks, as though
it has been turned on with the flick of a switch.
On such a morning a .22 caliber bullet in the left side

stopped Michael Turner's life six weeks short of his thirtieth birthday. Turner, a Parks Department security guard, was found slumped at the wheel of his patrol vehicle at 8 A.M. on July 15. He was working the midnight-to-eight duty, filling in for a man who was sick, and last made radio contact at 5:10 A.M. Police said a gunman had shot Turner at point-blank range under the armpit, the bullet penetrating a lung and his heart.

Turner, who was unarmed, was the first parks department employee to die in the line of duty. He was the sixth person murdered in the park since January.

·   ·   ·

An elderly man with a bare, bronzed chest and a scraggy straw hat stood on a green wooden bench I had come to regard as my own. In his hand was an imaginary baton that he used to summon a not so imaginary overture. His face was hidden under the hat, but the perspiration started to run down his arms, dripping onto the wooden slats of the bench, when Tchaikovsky's "1812" was in full flight. The music stopped abruptly and the man stopped in the frozen pose of a conductor.

"One more time," said the bare-chested man to the New York Philharmonic Orchestra, which was situated one hundred yards away across the Great Lawn. Simultaneously, almost as if he were a shimmering, heat-haze reflection of the man on the bench, conductor John Nelson waved his real baton. The orchestra swung into the overture's stirring crescendo, with rising strings, woodwinds, and brass. The orchestra, its members in T-shirts and shorts in the ninety-two-degree heat, was practicing for an open-air performance the same evening. The music died away after a final thud of percussion, and the old man put away his imaginary baton and said to the distant orchestra: "That'a do. . . ."

The musicians were departing as the first music-lovers reserved their patches of sand and grass for the concert, raising flags and banners to let their friends know where they had staked their musical claim. That night a man climbed on stage and grabbed the conductor. The man was dragged away by police who later reported he was protesting over the choice of the piece of music being played at the time—Rimsky-Korsakov's "Scheherazade." He liked Wagner.

·   •   •

A tourist from Maine was sitting with his girlfriend on the terrace of the boathouse cafeteria, which overlooks the boating lake. He saw the group of people with binoculars at the next table and inquired whether they were "into birds," as he put it.

"Well," he continued, "I was sitting here this morning and this big heron came by and settled right in front of us. I couldn't believe it and I said to my girlfriend here, 'That's like a great blue heron which we get in Maine.' But you wouldn't get such a bird in the middle of New York."

"Well, you can," Lambert replied, continuing that an entry for a great blue heron had been made in the bird sightings register. A Northern waterthrush, traditionally the first bird of the downward fall migration, was also recorded that day, July 27. I did not see the heron or the waterthrush but a hard day's birding rewarded me with a brown-headed cowbird with a youngster in tow. Although brought up by foster parents of another species, the young cowbird had recognized its own kind as soon as it was able to fly and fend for itself. I like to think the cowbird was one of the offspring of the cowbirds that I had seen in courtship in the spring. It was difficult to believe the fledgling had not been reared by the cowbird it was with. It worried the adult bird constantly, chasing it along branches and following the cowbird to the grass to search for food.

Although it was only two months since the northward migration petered out, the birds would soon be coming south again in large numbers. The fall migration is basically a mirror image of the one in spring, with the insect-eaters now coming first and the hardier birds arriving later.

A severe thunderstorm struck New York on July 28. Trees were felled and it rained all day, making the hunt for the waterthrush and another trumpeter of fall, the redstart, impossible. But next day I came across waterthrushes by the dozen and a single redstart, precisely on schedule. I paused to survey the rich green foliage of the park, layers of leaves ruffled by a slight northerly wind. Cicadas chirping, the plop of bullfrogs leaping into the boating lake—my mind could not grasp the harsh images of winter, the skeletal branches, the coating of snow, the ice on the reservoir, the Iceland gulls, the scaups, and the canvasback ducks coated with oil, coming to the park to die. The redstarts and waterthrushes could not endure a northern winter. Something told them the insects they feed on would soon be dying, and it was time to head south.

•   •   •

A blue jay was on a branch just above my head, peering down and making a gurgling sound that I thought might be part of a mating cry. The bird descended rapidly, brushing my head before I had time to duck. The jay, which had young about, dove twice more, causing me to throw up my arms to cover my head. I let out a yell. The jay's mate joined it in the attack, and I started to run, my body straightening from its crouched position as I picked up speed. Crash. After looking behind me at the jays, I had tripped over a root, banged my head against the ground and rolled beneath a linden, blood trickling from a nick across my left eyebrow. "Sir," said a little boy, who was half hidden behind the trunk of a tree. He had the supercilious, stern, head-cocked-back look of a child trying to be an adult. "I wouldn't be frightened of a mere bird. . . ."

The incident happened during a period when I was still telling my Africa stories, and I did not recount it at the boathouse. I had already been shamed by a mere plant, poison ivy. Lambert had pointed out its glossy, bottle-green leaves in spring, rising from the earth in sets of three. I said that someone who had entered crocodile-infested rivers, and climbed thorn trees in search of martial eagles' nests, would not be deterred by a plant, which in all probability would have no greater sting than the slight irritation caused by a brush with British stinging nettles.

"I'm immune to poison ivy," I joked, pushing aside a few sprigs of the plant to climb the steep bank of the Upper Lobe. I was only wearing a T-shirt, my arms exposed, and that night I thought I had contracted the tick-borne Rocky Mountain spotted fever. My arms swelled in red blotches, and I scratched and could not sleep. I got up to have a hot bath and sweated and itched some more. Next day I was fidgety. I could not hold my binoculars up to my eyes for more than a few seconds.

"What's wrong with you?" said Lambert, losing patience when he was trying to point out a chickadee's nest. "I think it's poison ivy," I replied.

"But I thought you were immune."

·   ·   ·

A blue jay, emitting an ecstatic cooing, rolled its body in a heap of dried leaves that had been overrun by ants. The jay then pushed its body and wings tight to the ground and watched, its beak gaping, as the ants crawled over its feathers, the ants tunneling amid the shafts and vanes. The blue jay antics were taking place off the Mall, and a man I suspected was a drug seller stopped to watch, and then asked me what was going on.

I explained it was a behavioral characteristic, common to many species of birds, which ornithologists call "anting." The ants release acids that deter parasites and are also believed to bring relief to skin made sore by the moult and the growth of new feathers at the end of summer. The drug seller had another, more concise term for anting. He called it a "fix."

· *August* ·

*T*he wind was listless and the only ripples on the boating lake were caused by the girl I had seen twice in winter, ice-skating and jogging. Now the girl, alone, was rounding the tip of the Point in a rowing boat. Her flaxen hair had been bleached by the sun and a yellow T-shirt hung loosely on a mahogany body. The rowing motion revealed slender but strong arms, the outline of pert breasts whose nipples pushed into the soft fabric of the T-shirt as she pulled on the oars. It was hot and the girl, maybe eighteen years of age, was perspiring gently. She laughed at a group of slightly younger teenage boys on Bow Bridge, who threatened to drop stones into the water to make a splash. Under the bridge she rowed, slowly, and she was soon lost in the glare of sunlight reflecting from her oar strokes.

In the boathouse cafeteria a man sat talking to himself, a middle-aged man in a neatly pressed navy blue suit, his striped shirt unbuttoned at the collar. People paid little attention to him and no one joined in his laughter, when he laughed at a joke he had told himself. At another table outside on the terrace, a man scolded a couple for feeding the pigeons.

"It's unhygienic," he said, the gray stubble on his chin moving as he spoke. He had taken off his holed leather shoes to reveal that he was not wearing socks. His feet were lined with dried dirt, like the tide mark on a beach, and the couple feeding the pigeons nervously sneaked a crumb to a sparrow that had landed on their table. The man saw them, and without looking up, uttered an obscenity into a cardboard cup that had a tea bag floating in it.

·　　　　·　　　　·

A kingbird hawked insects a few feet above the rowing boats on the lake, returning to a nearby linden after each sortie. When perching, the bird held an erect posture. He had a slight crest and his plumage was colored matte black on the head and back, whitish below. Kingbirds, members of the tyrant flycatcher family, were present in the park all summer but, by August 1, I had not determined whether they bred there.

A search for a kingbird nest, and a nagging concern about the mallard family threatened by the night heron, took me in the direction of the reservoir. Three remaining mallard chicks had lost their mother, but they appeared to be supporting themselves adequately and had grown to half-size, too big now for the heron to seriously consider them as prey. What had happened to the mother? Had she deserted the ducklings, or just lost track of them in a storm that had lashed the park in late July? Was she shot by a pellet gun aimed through the reservoir fence, or speared in a night-time encounter with a heron's bill? I would never know.

I had neglected the reservoir in the summer. But in August there was an interesting arrival in the low-slung shape of a double-crested cormorant, a fish-eating water bird with a snake neck and long bill, hooked at the tip. The cormorant, midway in size between a duck and a goose, dives for long periods in pursuit of fish. Unlike members of the duck family, the species does not have a biological process for oiling its feathers, to keep water from seeping into them, and so the cormorant has to dry its wings on exposed perches, standing like a black scarecrow. The cormorants are common on the coast during migration; they breed beyond Massachusetts, but visits to the reservoir by up to forty cormorants had only started occurring in recent years.

Lambert had told me to watch the reservoir periodically in mid-year because juvenile loons, too young to breed, had sometimes spent the summer there, but he did not have an explanation for the cormorants' recent arrival.

I had my own theory, in defiance of any esoteric explanation that might be advanced by a professional ornithologist at the American Museum of Natural History. It concerned a lone cormorant, heading south, who happened to cut inland and cross Manhattan. The clear waters of the reservoir looked inviting on a hot August afternoon and the cormorant decided to spiral down with the herring gulls, to investigate the park's marine world. The first underwater dive produced a meal of largemouth bass, and so the cormorant dried its wings on the exposed water pipeline and moved on to the park's other pools and lakes, an explorer, the Christopher Columbus of the avian world. The cormorant of this piece of whimsy discovered nine species of fish and a freshwater jellyfish, making a note of the fish so he could report back to his friends: pumpkin-seed, bluegill, golden shiner, yellow perch, banded killifish, black bullhead, brown bullhead, goldfish, and largemouth bass.

The goldfish were a surprise, easily detected in the murky waters of the boating lake. Honey bees are known to guide other members of their colonies to food sources, so why not the cormorant? Certainly, after I first saw the lone bird, numbers of cormorants were to appear in successive weeks.

·   ·   ·

Lambert told me the migration south would be a leisurely

affair, compared to spring, but during the final days of August and building up to mid-September there were wave days to almost equal those of May. As in early spring, the movement of birds through the park had started slowly. After the Northern waterthrushes and redstarts, the black-and-white warblers appeared in the first week of August. There were also increased numbers of birds I had observed all summer long in the park—night herons, grackles, robins and flickers, all moving south. The leaves on the trees now had a slightly jaded, tattered look like the wings of the butterflies that had laid eggs and were now preparing to die. The leaves were also turning a dark, dirty green before their transformation into shades of brown, red and gold during the fall.

But the weather continued hot in early August, causing the horses that haul the carriages around the lower part of the circular road to foam white and frothy at the bit, to struggle wearily up the slight gradients. Three horses whose lifetime job had been to pull the carriages had dropped dead on New York streets during summer and, on August 4, another beast of burden lay dead on Central Park South. The twelve-year-old carriage horse was covered by a blanket, and mothers led their children away. An autopsy later showed the horse's death was related to the heat. At the scene a summons was issued to the stable owner because the horse's log, to show how long it had worked on the days preceding its death, was not up to date. The other three horses' deaths had been caused by heat exhaustion.

Blue-winged and Canada warblers were the next insect-eaters to swarm through the park, and they brought with them a summer storm from the west that tore some of the posters carrying the face of murdered park guard Michael Turner from tree trunks (the police were offering fifteen thousand dollars for information leading to his murderer's conviction). The torrent on August 10 had created bathing pools in rock grooves for birds to wash in, and the storm had also spurred a squirrel to start building his winter nest in a willow. The nest was a mass of green vegetation camouflaged in the tree, but in winter it would stand out as a solid, if untidy, bundle in the crisscross of branches.

·   ·   ·

Intermittent rain did not deter thousands of schoolchildren from gathering in front of the Bandshell. A summer carnival for the city's underprivileged children had been organized by the Police Athletic League, and disco music boomed through the elms along the Mall. A giant map gave locations of where the street games were being played in the vicinity: "double dutch," hopscotch, tag, and hockey. And at a table manned by a plainclothes policeman there was a display to illustrate another kind of street activity with another kind of street language: "bennies," "block-busters," "coke," "brown sugar," "junk," and "joints." Laid out on the table was the paraphernalia of the drug cult, from syringes to razor blades, and after fingering a plastic poppy and a plastic marijuana plant, the kids in PAL-issue T-shirts moved on to another stall, which had free candy and helium balloons.

Many of the same kids were getting hooked two days later in the park. The New York Housing Authority was holding its annual fishing contest for four thousand children of tenants in its housing projects. More hooks were caught in young anglers' clothing and hair than in the waters of the boating lake, giving a break to several thousand fish that had been slipped into the lake for the occasion by the State Conservation Department.

·   ·   ·

After searching all summer for evidence of kingbirds nesting, I was now convinced I had seen a family party of the flycatchers, although they were some distance away, beyond the Point. I found the kingbirds in the trees where I had seen the ruby-throated hummingbird in May. Two noisy, anxious youngsters were pursuing their parents, demanding food. As the nesting season was closing, I had a tally of sixteen birds breeding in the park and possibly four others.

Forty-two species are known to have nested in the park successfully since it opened. The birds I found nesting were: mallard, mourning dove, downy woodpecker, kingbird, blue jay, black-capped chickadee, tufted titmouse, mockingbird, catbird, robin, starling, house sparrow, common grackle, Northern cardinal, house finch, and feral pigeon. The other possible breeders were American kestrel, common crow, song sparrow, and cowbird.

The flickers had not made it finally and among the birders there was antipathy toward the starlings. So there was something to celebrate on August 14 when a female kestrel was observed with a starling in her talons. I had not heard of a kestrel taking a bird as big as a starling before. Again the woods fell silent as the kestrel came over, and it was some time before the usually noisy starlings struck up their rising one-note whistle call.

The same day the kestrel struck, the body of the park's seventh murder victim was discovered under low bushes where ovenbirds had returned. The victim, shot once above the right ear near West Sixty-third Street, was dressed in a waiter's uniform. Immediately, a team of twenty-five detectives started to canvass restaurants near the park in an attempt to identify the man.

By mid-August I had seen ten warblers, a warblerlike bird called a red-eyed vireo, and a gnatcatcher, which meant the downward migration was fully under way. At times the park would be overrun by Canada warblers, in far greater numbers than I had seen in the spring. I had read that some birds varied their migration route on the southward journey, which could explain the increase in numbers of certain species and the absence of others. Certainly, one warbler, the Connecticut, is only seen in the park in the fall.

The curtain came down on the summer music program on August 16 when the last open-air symphony concert took place in the park. The Indian conductor Zubin Mehta took the New York Philharmonic through pieces by Bartok, Copland, and Mussorgsky. By intermission the sky was pink from the remnants of the setting sun and, high up, on pointed wings and moving fast, what looked like a common nighthawk swerved after insects.

·   ·   ·

"Birding can make a hermit of one," wrote Lambert in mid-July. "A hermit in a crowd." He explained through the uneven keys of an old typewriter that he had not seen me, or many of the other birders, in the park recently because he had been visiting lesser used areas looking for nests.

The hermit metaphor again made me curious about Lambert's life outside the family of birders and birds. I could not confront him directly, which I considered presumptuous or just plain impertinent, and during our conversations there was never a moment when I could slip in a casual inquiry about, say, his marital status, without obviously taking our discussion off at a tangent. Finally, I took the easy way out and asked one of the other birders what Lambert did for a living, as a starting point to understanding more about him.

My informant was selected carefully, someone who appreciated the difference between curiosity and prying. He was a former journalist, who now loaded newspapers on trucks on weekends so he could spend the rest of his time bird watching.

"Well, Lambert works during the weekends on Staten Island," the former journalist replied after some thought. "That's the closest I ever got myself."

•   •   •

As the migration of insect-eating birds starts to peak, it is time to concentrate less on the woods and to scan the sky for birds of prey. The hawks and falcons follow the warblers south, preying on them during the journey, and the best place to search for the raptors is from the Bow Bridge, which offers an uncluttered view of the airways.

But on August 19 there was a migration of a different kind. Certain butterfly species, particularly the monarchs, also move south, and on this day the sky was full of the satin-winged insects. The butterflies spread their orange, black-edged wings upward and rose in thermals, spiraling so high that they were lost to sight. The streets of the city were also full of the migrating monarchs, and in the final days of August I saw a particularly fine specimen flying along the tracks of the elevated Lexington Avenue subway line through the South Bronx. The butterfly's short life was brought to an abrupt halt by a Number 4 train moving north.

I, too, was moving north, against the flow of the monarchs, in the latter part of August. A business trip took me to the Canadian capital of Ottawa, and I had an opportunity to see firsthand why the downward migration starts so early. By August 22 chill winds were already blowing from the Arctic, and the leaves on the maples in downtown Ottawa were dying. Wasps were gripped in death throes on the sidewalk, and cedar waxwings traveled along the banks of the Ottawa River searching for berries, as they would do all winter. Over the river in Quebec, Cape May and chestnut-sided warblers, and redstarts, headed toward the United States and warmer weather. I arrived back in New York on August 28 to catch a wave day. The cold front from Canada had pushed the temperature down to fifty-nine degrees and the brisk northwesterly winds brought at least eighteen species of warbler with them. The park was alive with birds. A new species for the year, a yellow-breasted chat, was seen on the Point. I missed the chat, a skulking bird, which is the largest of the warbler family and rare in the park; but I picked up my first thrush of the fall, a veery. The wave continued the next day and was well-timed for Lambert and Sarah, who were leading their third bird walk of the year. I spent an hour studying a batch of Cape May warblers on the Point and wanted to believe they were the same birds I had seen in Canada, although the chances of that were a million to one. Loose flocks of cedar waxwings also came through the park, their cicadalike call harmonizing with the crickets.

      •   •   •

The scribbled sign said: "Snake poet—25 cents." Along with an open shoebox, the sign lay at the base of a tree that contained a woman in her early twenties, who was reading poetry to a small, silent crowd looking up at her. Around her neck was a very long and very thick boa constrictor, which kept trying to slide away. The girl, dressed in a black leotard and bright red ballet shoes, raised her voice as she wrestled with the serpent, which featured so strongly in her poetry. I sympathized with the snake, carpet-patterned and so eager to explore the boughs of the tree. I did not like the poetry, either.

      •   •   •

Billy lacked his usual sparkle. There was dust on his coat, and his head hung wearily. It was early morning on the last day of August, and I thought Billy might have been hunting all night, without success. Young birds that had been easy prey all summer were now flying on strong wings and were as hard to catch as their parents. So Billy was grateful for the handout of fish, raw and fresh and pungent-smelling and flaking in my fingers. His nose twitched as he caught the aroma; he rose slowly to his feet, yawning, lowering his head and coming straight to me without hesitation. He bit hard and swallowed hurriedly, and on the second bite he sank a tooth into my finger, drawing blood. I flinched. He backed off. But the smell of the fresh fish drew him to me again. A breakthrough, he had taken food from my hand, and within two weeks he would come running when I called.

•   •   •

In February, the ice on the boating lake near West Seventy-fifth Street had looked firm and safe enough when thirteen-year-old Enzo DiBello and his younger brother, Victor, ventured on to it, gingerly at first. Then it cracked under them; that sickening crack, loss of balance, freezing water making the boys gasp for breath. Fifty people, hearing the boys' screams, looked on helplessly until two bystanders edged their way across the ice toward the struggling brothers. Although the ice had started to give way under the rescuers, they managed to stand upright in the muddy water and grab hold of the boys.

Victor, nine on his last birthday, wrapped in a blanket, his face purple with cold, would never again see the lake covered in ice. On August 31, chased by Enzo in a game of tag, he ran under a bus near their home in Ozone Park, Queens, and was killed outright.

· *September* ·

*H*umid on the first day of September, a greasy, perspira-
tion-pulling humidity, which New York City had escaped for
much of the cool summer. In the sheltered gullies of the
park the air hung thick like damp laundry. The insects appeared to be suspended and trapped in moisture, and the
warblers dropped in slow flight, wing and tail feathers outstretched, to snap at the midges and mosquitoes as they
passed. Parula, Canada, and black-and-white warblers, and
redstarts shared a tight space where the stream in the Indian
Cave melts into the boating lake. The warblers adopted the
same routine during the downward journey, seeking safety
in numbers during the uncertain, tortuous course of migration, knowing instinctively that the birds of prey were also
on the move, just behind them.

The migration of bird watchers to the park was very
much like the movement of birds at this time of the year—
casual, not as prolific as in April and May. During spring
birders had taken "sick" days from work so they could spend
time in the park, or the more honest ones had made an
arrangement to arrive later at the office or the workshop.
The "hooky" syndrome, that feeling of elation derived from
cheating the system to do something you really want to do,
illicitly, was absent and, as a result, bird watching became

more of a sober affair. It takes more skill and stamina to bird watch in the fall; this might explain the drop in numbers of people birding. Most birds have lost their spring mating plumage, and the warblers become confusing—a group of them are technically referred to as "confusing fall warblers" —because females, moulting males and juveniles of many species look similar. One birder who did not lose any enthusiasm was Lambert, who now carried a flicker's feather of yellow-gold in his hat. But he was torn between his twin passions of birds and butterflies.

The hardcore Central Park birding fraternity numbers about fifty. There is no stereotype, or composite picture of a birder, although people who regard bird watching as an eccentricity like to believe there is. Among the birders is a man who talks loudly because he spent his working life in a railroad switching yard, a viola player with the New York Philharmonic Orchestra who has an ear for birdsong, and a used car salesman who frequently warned me about "lemons." Another birder, until he retired, was a policeman and another, until he became deceased, a bank robber.

The bank robber story, a favorite for rainy days when the bird watchers are confined to the boathouse: the bank robber carried a little black book in his back pocket in which was recorded his life list of birds spotted. He told other bird watchers he was a writer and for long periods he was not seen in the park. He was traveling for research purposes, he said. Then one day a birder saw a news item in a newspaper about a man shot dead in the process of robbing a bank in San Francisco. The San Francisco police, so the story goes, returned the robber's life list to the boathouse.

It is raining. The bank robber story is finished and now comes a second favorite: a tale about the policeman birder who, when he was wearing his uniform, was one of the most popular people in the park. Once the Emperor of Japan paid a visit to Central Park, for reasons which are obscure now.

But his visit coincided with the bird migration and the policeman birder went on duty with his binoculars, commandeered a rowboat and, from the center of the boating lake, spent the afternoon scanning willows for warblers. One of the top officers of the New York force saw the policeman birder and later commended him for his "initiative." The officer thought the policeman was looking for snipers.

One more bird watching story, this time my own. It is mid-morning and the retired couple who linger at the boathouse waiting for an escort of birders have accompanied me into the Ramble. I explain that I have limited time because I must be at work within a couple of hours.

"You're lucky," says the wife. "You could be retired."

·   ·   ·

A blue jay in the lower branches of a plane tree on Fifth Avenue screamed at people sitting in temporary bleachers erected on the sidewalk. The jay had been trying to feed on acorns on the other side of the park's wall, but people climbing the wall to reach the rear entrance of the bleachers were disturbing the bird, a juvenile from this year's brood, who believed it owned the park.

The crowd had gathered between East Sixty-second and Sixty-third Streets to see the finish of the Fifth Avenue Mile on September 4. A voice boomed over loudspeakers that the runners were "off" at Eighty-second Street. The crowd fell silent but the blue jay started up again. The spectators ignored it and craned their necks to look along the street. Two police motorcycles, blue lights flashing, appeared in the distance. One hundred yards behind them was the thin line of some of the fastest milers in the world. Lanky, muscled legs pounded tar, which had been warmed by an afternoon of sunshine, and a block from the finish Tom Byers of the United States kicked clear of the rest of the field. Shoulder-length blond hair coursing behind him, Byers clocked 3 minutes, 51.35 seconds to win the straight mile. "He'd have run faster if he got his hair cut," said a New York cop holding back the spectators. Watching the race, and the television circus that accompanies such a sporting event, I was not to know a rare Connecticut warbler was working its way through the low bushes that surround the west side of the Point Lobe. A mourning warbler, equally rare, was seen in the same location. The television cables running along Fifth Avenue to a central control point in the park were being wound in when I finally wandered to the boathouse to check the bird register. My heart raced like Tom Byers's at the mile's finish when I saw the entry for the two species. I scoured the shrubbery around the Point Lobe for an hour without success. The Connecticut and mourning warblers would come to represent a frustrating fall and my good fortune of the spring would not be repeated. Although I had been in the park virtually every day since mid-July—with only a week's break in August—vital birds, which I needed to make the one hundred fifty target, eluded me. Bad luck stalked me for the entire month, and the only new species for September was a Philadelphia warbler—my first new bird since I recorded the cedar waxwings in May.

The waxwings were now common on the Point where the two thousand fruit trees planted during the winter were rich with berries. The waxwings and the robins swallowed the berries whole, but I noticed the warblers—I counted eight species on September 4—merely pierced the skins and sucked out the juices. Although warblers are basically insect-eaters, they supplement their diet with other available food in the fall. The flickers also enjoyed the fruit. Ungainly, they waded across clusters of berries. The flickers, the biggest members of the woodpecker family represented in the park, are built and balanced to cling to tree trunks. They looked ill at ease amid the fruit and appeared in danger of toppling out of the branches at any moment. In contrast, the chick-adees were masters of the berry-eating technique. A chick-adee hung upside down from a clump of berries, picked one and then fell with the berry in its beak before righting itself in mid-air and landing on a nearby branch. The bird then gripped the berry in its feet and stabbed at it with needle bill. At the tip of the Point an empidonax flycatcher had left the trees to perch on a rock jutting into the water. The flycatcher flitted across the lake to catch mosquitoes hover-ing a few inches above the surface, and then the bird plunged into vegetation behind the rock to spear a cabbage-white butterfly. There are five species of empidonax flycatcher, and they are virtually identical in appearance, song being the only reliable guide to identification. Al-though I had a willow flycatcher pointed out for me in the spring I did not put it on my list because I was not satisfied I could identify the species myself. Now in the fall, the flycatchers did not sing, and this one on the Point would elude identification.

It was a balmy, pleasant early evening, and I lingered in the park. Hundreds of people had gathered around the Bel-vedere Lake to watch the folk dancing in front of the King Jagiello statue or to be entertained by mime artists and busk-ers. The cold, gray granite of the newly restored Belvedere Castle loomed over the lake, a romantic ghost from the days of the park's construction. The backdrop of setting sun high-lighted the castle's turrets and battlements, and town pi-geons arrived to roost in crevices in the outcrop of rock on which the castle is built. A barn owl had once used this roost for a winter, but pigeons unable to forget their roots had taken it over as a nesting site in spring and a roost in the other seasons—in the same way that their ancestors colonize rocky sites in Europe.

The start of the hawk migration was signaled by two majestic ospreys during the first two days of September but

I missed the birds. On September 5 I decided to spend the whole afternoon watching for hawks and, at the same time, get on line for tickets to "A Midsummer Night's Dream," the last performance of the summer at the Delacorte Theater. The performances are free but an all-afternoon wait is necessary to obtain tickets. On my way to the theater I had passed a green heron, standing on a floating plank of wood, jealously guarding his fishing ground in the Upper Lobe, and now I guarded my place in a line of theater-goers, which stretched around the whole of the Great Lawn. I had a bottle of French red wine, a picnic lunch, a book and binoculars for hawk watching, and I could not think of a better way to spend an afternoon. More than one thousand people, all waiting for tickets, were camped out on the Great Lawn; all afternoon they were pestered by vendors selling soda, beer, hot dogs, marijuana joints, and cocaine. Among these was a fat man with odd socks, a dirty vest, and shorts. He carried a cardboard box tied with a string handle so that it resembled a suitcase, and he carefully placed this on the grass when he stopped at each group of theater enthusiasts.

"I'm a poet," he said through a white beard that followed the line of his round face and then stopped abruptly at his bronzed bald head. "If you buy one of my poems it'll bring you luck." When the poet sensed he had not caught the customers' attention, he added quickly: "Luck, and two years' immunity from herpes."

·   ·   ·

The vagrant who knows all about unemployment had found a day-old *New York Times* in a trash bin near the boathouse. He was reading it on one of the wooden benches outside the cafeteria and he called to me as I walked past.

"See what I told you about when you said 'Go find a job.' " The finance pages recorded that unemployment was well over ten million, or nine percent of the country's work-force.

During infrequent encounters with the vagrant, who told me his name was Chuck, I had learned more about him than I knew of Lambert, my friend. Chuck had come to New York from a steel town in Pennsylvania, searching for work. The steel mill in a town he did not identify had closed, and he shed Pennsylvania and a wife and two children to come to "the big apple."

"Actually, drink was also something to do with it," he once said when he took me to see a night heron he believed was building a nest. He said he had a brother in New York who sometimes helped him out when times got tough, but he had done a couple of odd jobs during the spring and summer to keep him in food.

"The idea is to get an apartment but I can't get enough for a deposit. Once I get a regular job I'll be settled."

Regular jobs, however, were few and far between. "I don't want to be nosy," I said on the morning we surveyed the financial pages of *The New York Times.* "But why do you live in the park? Why don't you go to a shelter?" There was a contemplative silence. " 'Cause I got pride and respect for m'self. I served in Nam and I can look after m'self and I ain't afraid of the wild, the open. 'Cause that's what I want. . . ."

With that the conversation ended.

· · ·

Strong northeasterly winds and a clear night followed by a sunny day brought another wave day on September 7. Tra-ditionally, the migration peaks around mid-September, but it appeared the cold weather in Canada in late August had spurred an early movement. Highlights of the day were the first of the fall's red-breasted nuthatches and a scarlet tanager. The tanager, a female in dull-green plumage with

blackish wings, gorged herself on black cherry fruit in the
Indian Cave. The first male black-throated blue warbler also
arrived, along with twelve other species of warbler. Later I
would find the Turkey oaks near the reservoir alive with
black-throated blues, some of them sweeping down to pick
up insects that had landed on the warm cinder path surrounding the water. These birds, realizing the joggers were
a nuisance but not a threat to them, perched on the reservoir fence and timed their dives for insects between the
passing of runners. I do not think there is a more striking
bird than this black, blue, gray, and white warbler. When I
see one I am reminded of a story Lambert tells of a birder
who was so besotted with the species that he had his car
sprayed in the same color scheme.

A survey of Central Park conducted during 1982 by a
group of urban forestry students revealed there were 24,595
trees whose trunks were more than six inches in diameter,
the biggest being an English elm planted by the Prince of
Wales in 1860 and the oldest a bur oak dating back two
hundred and fifty or three hundred years. Many of these six
hundred species of trees were now shedding their fruits of
berries and nuts, and in certain places the ground-feeding
birds like robins and mourning doves were joined by flickers. Sometimes the ground was alive with the three species;
the robins and doves perfectly matched in placid tempera-
ment, but the flickers agitated and active, quicker to fly. I
suppose the flickers, although often seen digging in and
feeding on the ground, felt vulnerable out of the trees.

Gentle northeasterly winds had blown for three continuous days by September 8 and again two ospreys soared high
in thermals at noon. One of the birders telephoned me at my
office on Times Square to tell me about the fish-eating raptors. Immediately I looked into the sky over midtown Manhattan, directly to the south of the park, but I could not see
the birds. I had last seen a majestic osprey, a bird not unlike

a bald eagle, in the Central African country of Malawi, so cosmopolitan are the birds. The osprey in Africa had hovered for a few seconds when it sighted a fish, its legs dangling, before dropping to the water, disappearing in a cloud of spray. On rising, with the fish carried head forward, the osprey had shaken the water off its plumage while in flight, then flown to an exposed branch where it consumed its catch. Seeing the osprey fishing had been one of my most thrilling sights in nature, and I could not believe such a bird, with a six-foot wingspan, was flying commonly over New York City.

·   ·   ·

I went to the park after work hoping to see an osprey before sunset. All I found was a grackle making the most of the rapidly disappearing number of insects. The grackle perched in the willows over the Upper Lobe and casually picked off the butterflies and moths fluttering in the hot, stagnant air caught in this steeply sided corner of the boat lake. A big, juicy-bodied cabbage-white butterfly went by and the grackle lunged at it, flycatcherlike. But before he could return to his perch he dropped the insect. With shattered wing, the butterfly tumbled down and down and the grackle swooped after it, trying desperately to grab the insect before it hit the water. The grackle was slow and the cabbage-white settled on a bed of aquatic vegetation covering the lobe, flapping painfully. The grackle, raising its feathers in anger, stood on a log at the water's edge, croaking loudly as the butterfly started to sink below the weeds. The commotion attracted a male scarlet tanager, now back in lime-green plumage after summer transformation to red, and the tanager stayed on to take advantage of the supply of insects discovered by the grackle.

A red maple at the circular route was turning to a color

of bright red not unlike the scarlet tanager's summer plumage. The color change, speeded by a dry spell in August and early September, started in the lowest branches of the tree. On the branches overhanging the road, however, the leaves were withered and crinkled like a thousand tightly clenched fists. The leaves were being poisoned by auto exhaust fumes. Already I had seen evidence of New York's pollution by studying the obelisk called Cleopatra's Needle erected in the park near the Metropolitan Museum of Art. For three thousand years the obelisk had stood relatively unharmed in the dry desert climate of Egypt but now deterioration by both chemical and natural weathering made its hieroglyphics indecipherable in places. The erosion of the needle was particularly noticeable from the southwest side where, I assume, most of the wind bringing particles of dust and harmful chemical pollutants came from. But the needle was not living and did not emit a feeling of distress and pain as the maple did. The maple was crippled down one side, layers of contorted, dry leaves giving shape to the invisible poison that rises from thousands of vehicles passing daily under the tree's branches.

•   •   •

Shadows were growing longer by mid-afternoon; the gradual closing in of daylight, which lets you know summer is ending and soon it will be cold and dark by 4:30 P.M., and when you wake up next morning it will still be dark. The prolific movement of birds through the park would drop off dramatically; Billy would have to go farther and farther for food, increasing the risk of being caught in the cat-catcher's trap, of eating poison laid for the rats or of being killed by an automobile on the circular drive. I feared someday finding his body by the roadside. I knew he sometimes wandered across the circular drive because I had seen him a few times on the east side of the park. I had called his name on these occasions but he did not respond. I think he only associated me with the Ramble and was shy of approaching someone who could be a stranger.

Mist covered the park on September 13 but I made out the shape of a male belted kingfisher hurrying through the tulip trees edging the boating lake. A well-fed woodchuck ran across the path leading to the Point, and I wondered whether it was the same animal I had seen in the Indian Cave at the end of April. It must have been, I suppose, and now the woodchuck had moved to a clump of rocks on the Point where Chuck, the vagrant from Pennsylvania, had built a home of cardboard. Chuck told me that park rangers had evicted him from the bird sanctuary when he had tried to build a temporary home there, ready for the winter. His new house was hidden under an overhanging rock and shielded by a black cherry. I had stumbled on it by accident and promised Chuck I would not point out its location to the rangers.

I found Chuck most mornings sitting under the willows at the Point Lobe, a short distance from his home, and when he was not reading discarded newspapers with yesterday's unemployment figures he stared at the water. He pretended not to notice me after I had discovered his home so I honored his privacy. He also lost interest in the birds that came to drink and feed at the lobe, and he would not bother to look up at the noisy blue jays frequently mobbing night and green herons in the willow.

·   ·   ·

Sitting on my favorite park bench I thought about many things in 1982, but my thoughts were mainly taken up with two subjects: retracing the course of my life and the topic of evolution. Contemplating evolution, especially, took up much of my time when I was not actually chasing birds. Sometimes I could watch birds from the bench and ponder evolution at the same time, as I did one Saturday afternoon in September when I observed a mad-eyed thrasher under a copper beech. Charles Darwin's theory of evolution seemed so obvious now, and I wondered how I would have felt about creation one hundred and fifty years ago when Darwin was ferreting about the Galapagos Islands and most other people still believed all creatures great and small were created as is, plain and simple, by God.

I am watching a thrasher, thinking this bird could have evolved just to feed and reproduce in the fall, so perfectly does its warm brown plumage, its brown-speckled chest on buff, merge with the freshly fallen leaves. Later, on the Point, I find the three members of the thrasher family—the thrasher, the mockingbird, and the catbird—in one location, and I now start to think about coexistence and harmony: the mockingbird feeding on berries in a black cherry, the catbird crunching a moth larva it had prised from a dead knotweed stem under the tree, and a thrasher turning leaves on the ground. Perhaps Olmsted and Vaux had studied the "mocker" trio, diverse in plumage but sharing lovely songs, when they drew up their plan for the park. They named the plan Greensward and set out to cater to different levels of human activity and recreation in the same space, the bridle paths, footpaths, and carriage ways all going to the same place, sharing the same locations, but never clashing, never crossing each other on the same level. But the bridges and embankments to make this concept possible had been created with humans in mind; the animal kingdom of the park had evolved over millions of years to acquiesce in nature's architecture.

•   •   •

With the bulk of migrating passerines, or perching birds,

already past, the birders were anticipating the next phase of the migration: the arrival of the waterfowl.

Throughout the third week of September numbers of mallards and black ducks had built up on the Belvedere Lake bringing the promise of other species. The mallards— reaching more than one hundred in number on some days —found unexpected competition. A group of model boat enthusiasts had abandoned the Conservatory Pond for the lake, and a Second World War battleship one afternoon declared hostilities against a small group of ducks.

·　　·　　·

A man out walking his dog lay dead on the west side on September 16. The dog sat by the body of forty-year-old Richard Sperandio, on a leash that was still wrapped around his master's cold wrist. Sperandio had been shot in an area of the park between 104th and 105th Streets and police struggled to find a motive for the killing. Detectives even considered the possibility that Sperandio's dog had lunged at someone, and that person had taken umbrage.

·　　·　　·

The temperature touched eighty degrees on September 18 but even an oriole picking at berries on the Point could not feed an illusion of endless summer. Dead leaves crunched underfoot and the birds of early winter were reclaiming the park. A winter wren, stub-tailed and tame, and then a fine male ruby-crowned kinglet arrived at the Upper Lobe. On the bridle path I came across another winter bird, a white-throated sparrow, and all that was needed was a junco and a fox sparrow to seal summer in a capsule of memory.

Gray squirrels had taken over a hole in a Turkey oak where bees had nested earlier in the summer and were using it as a store for winter food. And, above, ospreys and sharp-shinned hawks sailed over but I missed them again. I began to wonder whether I should spend more time looking up at the sky and concentrate less on what went on immediately around me. Did I need to stop, yet again, to observe the lonely man, khaki shirt and knapsack, standing, as always, under the pin oak on the west side? He had his camera out but, as usual, was not filming anything or anybody. He merely stood shuffling from side to side, but with a shuffle of contentment, a relaxed, easy shuffle devoid of nervousness or paranoia. The alternative to those long days in the park was probably a dingy apartment in the city somewhere that never caught the sun and never trapped people's laughter and held it for a second like the embrace of the gentle and reassuring oaks. This man was not a "crazy" like so many of the people who claim one spot as their own in the park. He had contact, although tenuous, with other park users. Many joggers and cyclists recognized him and gave a smile or a nod of their heads to say hello and the man smiled back.

In the red-brick building, which houses a carousel, a man in his fifties sat astride a black and white wooden horse. The horse slowly rose and fell to the organ music and the grey-haired man rose and fell with it. He did not have a child with him and none would claim him later, after he had enough of the ride and looked for a stick of cotton candy.

Drizzle, northeasterly winds and a sharp drop in temperature coincided with an article in *The New York Times* warning of another severe winter. It could be the coldest winter this century, a number of meteorologists were quoted as saying, and they explained that billions of tiny parasols—drops of sulfuric acid released by volcanic eruptions—were shielding the earth from the sun. I cast my thoughts back to the last winter, the freak blizzard in April that left flickers and robins dead in the snow. The flickers this day, hundreds of them, were feeding on the berries that had fallen to the ground. As I walked through the Ramble I would count twenty at a time.

·   ·   ·

Among the water birds there are few as stately, as regal as the grebes. These avians, which are ducklike but unrelated to ducks, are considered the most perfectly adapted to water of all birds. Grebes not only feed, sleep, and court on water, but they also carry downy young on their backs in piggyback fashion. The bird register recorded two pied-billed grebes on the reservoir on September 22, but by the time I reached the location the grebes had flown, probably to another fresh water location because this species avoids salt water estuaries and the sea. I was bitterly disappointed because I am fond of grebes and particularly wanted to see this species. The pied-billed grebes are the smallest of the family in North America, stocky birds with stout bills, which look as though they are made of lead and have been flattened in a vise. I changed my routine next day, going to the reservoir first instead of heading straight into the Ramble as I had done since the end of spring. But my luck was not to change, nothing interesting was on the water except for gulls. The juvenile ring-billed gulls, which had stayed in the New York area all summer, were waiting for their up-country cousins to arrive in November. Next year it would be the turn of these youngsters, now more white than brown, to join the rigorous routine of migration, finding mates and rearing young.

·   ·   ·

Rain fell heavily along Fifth Avenue, hitting the road with a splatter and rising again in a fractured mushroom of sparkling light. A wind whipped sodden leaves from the London plane trees, and they fell black against the light. I was walking home from work at about 9 P.M., a hard day at the office and five beers inside me, when I paused at an entrance to the park in the Sixties. Too dangerous to venture in, black and foreboding; the trees, still heavy in thick leaf, obscuring the few lights there are in the park that work. I saw a black and white cat and realized it was Billy. He darted across the footpath about twenty yards into the park, more shadow than cat. But he turned as I called out and I caught the pattern on his face, his wild, wide eyes. Then he was off again, leaving me to dodge the suspicious glance of a policeman sheltering in a glass booth on the other side of the road.

The northeast wind that brought the rain also carried a rare golden-winged warbler and a gray-cheeked thrush to the Ramble. Both birds would have been new ones for the year but I missed them. I consoled myself that the thrush is not much to look at, not like his elegant cousin, the wood thrush, and the woods were now full of these. I had only seen one of the species in the spring and now I could see three or four at a time in the Ramble. The wood thrush is probably the most underrated of birds in terms of beauty. Birders are usually too busy chasing rarities to focus binoculars on the thrush and study its sublety of plumage. The thrush appears to have brown spots on a buff breast, but when it is viewed closely these are not spots at all but chevrons. The wood thrush stands smaller than its abundant relative, the robin, and his warm brown back merges into chestnut on the crown.

·   ·   ·

A vagrant insisted on trying to reach the lions at the zoo, pressing his face against the bars of their cages. Zoo keepers chased the man away several times but he returned each time. The vagrant had a vacant look to his brown eyes, a hint of despair, and when the keepers finally asked him if he needed help, the derelict looked into the distance and muttered, "You have to get close to the animals."

·   ·   ·

A horse chestnut tree embodied the message of fall, somber and grim, a chill wind of winter already touching the yellow-gold leaves, which turned under themselves at the edges, tired and ready to surrender to the next cold blast. A female towee, chestnut brown and active, joined two thrashers thrashing for insects amid the dead horse chestnut leaves and, in the tree itself, a ruby-crowned kinglet arrived, a male with spikes of red showing through the moss-green feathers of his head. Above the tree, waves of blue jays went over to the south and I followed one batch through my binoculars, losing them somewhere over the zoo.

·   ·   ·

The body of the vagrant who wanted to get close to the animals lay in the polar bear cage. The sun had just started to poke along the cross streets slicing the East Sixties, shedding zebra stripes of light up the shadowed Fifth Avenue. The body was lying partly in the wading pool of the cage and it had deep gashes to the head, neck, chest and arms. Skandy the 1,200-pound eleven-foot bear was close by. Zoo guards reported the vagrant, dressed only in a shirt and blue jeans, had twice been led out of the zoo by a watchman during the night. But he had been determined to enter the cage. He had scaled a ten-foot spiked fence enclosing the zoo, a five-foot fence surrounding the open-topped cage and then the twelve-foot cage itself.

•   •   •

A palm warbler, the first warbler I had seen in the spring, was feeding at the Point on September 27, but the birders gathering in the boathouse cafeteria had other things to discuss. One of them reported finding dozens of warblers each morning at the base of an office tower in midtown Manhattan. The glass building, its thousands of windows edged with silver and white, was illuminated at night, and this appeared to be a factor in the death of the migratory birds. In mist and low cloud, and disoriented by the dazzling light, it appeared confused birds were either flying into the building or trying to land, exhausted, on its smooth sides. From the time Manhattan's skyline first started to rise straight and fast like a plantation of young pines, the tall buildings have proven a deathtrap for migrating birds. John Bull records in his *Birds of the New York Area* that the Empire State Building was a notorious hazard until the 1960's when the management shut off a stationary all-night beacon during migrations. On a night in September 1948, 212 birds of thirty species were killed hitting the building; and after a rainy night in the same month in 1953 at least 130 birds died there. The birders mulled over these statistics and agreed it would be impossible to ask the owners of every high rise building in the city to turn off their lights.

"We'll just have to wait for the birds to evolve a navigational system for avoiding the lights," one of them said, half jokingly.

"And how long will that take?" asked another.

"Oh, about twenty-five thousand years," said Lambert, and no one could tell if he was joking or not.

•   •   •

The vagrant found dead in the zoo was identified next day

as Conrado Mones, a twenty-nine-year-old former biology
teacher from Cuba. Mones had come to the United States
sixteen months earlier in search of the American dream. He
had spent the first six months studying English because he
wanted to continue teaching but his job hunt had been fruitless. Mones worked at a gas station for a time but his friends
said he had started to act erratically in recent months, giving
up his job and occasionally spending nights on the streets.
Now he lay on a slab at the city morgue.

.   .   .

The fast and direct flight of a tree swallow carried the message for the insect-eating birds that it was finally time to
leave New York City. I only caught a glimpse of the swallow
and someone else had to identify it for me. It was brownish,
an immature, with buff belly and less of a forked tail than the
barn swallow. The swallow was one of six species which
could have had a place on my list, but I was reluctant to put
any of the six down because I was not absolutely sure about
their identification. The other birds were the olive-sided
flycatcher, Eastern pewee, a willow and least flycatcher, and
a night hawk. A bird that did not need a second opin-
ion was a male junco, which arrived with a female on the
same day as the swallow, September 28. The pair of juncos would be followed by hundreds of others in the next
few days. The wind was blowing strongly from the south
but five species of warbler arrived in the park, including
a magnolia and a batch of redstarts. There was also
another gray-cheeked thrush reported but, needless to
say, I missed it.

Another fall arrival was a lone yellow-bellied sapsucker,
noisily scaling a tree trunk near the Azalea Pond. The sapsucker heralded the arrival of possibly thirty or forty of his
species in the next few days, and I would get tired of seeing
what is normally a difficult bird to see in the park.

•   •   •

In the last days of September Rita Serrano tried to claim the torn body of her boyfriend, Conrado Mones, from the city morgue so that he could have a decent burial. Rita, with whom Conrado had lived until he wandered out onto the streets, was told she needed more money than she had. A funeral director had to be hired to bury the body in someplace other than the municipal potter's field on Hart Island, and funeral directors came expensive, she was told.

The leaves of the pin oaks had started to turn the color of claret, and the woods were becoming largely deserted of birds compared with the first day of September. Only an invasion of grackles made it obvious that the migration was still taking place. Hundreds of grackles swarmed over the ground on the west side, which was covered with the acorns of pin oaks, a favorite food. Although some of the grackles had lost their long, wedge-shaped tails in the fall moult, they still had traces of the species' gaudy purple-black plumage, tinged with bottle-green.

Warm and balmy. The sun about to fall behind the West Side and vanish beyond New Jersey. I am on my favorite bench, thinking about Darwin and his theory of evolution, again. I am looking at a bullfrog on a stone at the edge of the Belvedere Lake, and I am reminded that one of the birders has met a wildlife biologist in the park who is doing a survey of the mammals, amphibians, and reptiles. The bullfrogs, sensing the lake's water is getting colder, are less inclined to leave their sunning spots now, and they take an added risk to steal a last ray of sunlight before it is time for them to hibernate.

Early in the year I had considered the park an oasis, but I have come to see it as an island, perhaps like the Galapagos where specific species, adapted to the park, might evolve. Darwin would be interested, if he were around, in something the birder recounted. The wildlife biologist had said that unusual patterning had become fixed in the population of bullfrogs at the Belvedere Lake, patterning you would not find in bullfrogs elsewhere. I am thinking, on my park bench, that Central Park could have its own species of bull-frog in twenty thousand years. And there are other possibili-ties; even a human subspecies evolving in the park—*Homo sapiens Central Park.* The gene pool would come from the hundreds of people lingering, like the bullfrogs, to catch the sun on this balmy evening; most of them park freaks like myself who are reluctant to enter the city simply because they are reluctant to leave the park. My own favorite park people are about. Lambert is chasing the last of the swallow-tail butterflies in the Ramble, the lonely figure of the oaks is standing under his pin oak, Chuck from Pennsylvania is at home with yesterday's unemployment figures and the flax-en-haired girl who skates and jogs and rows is now watching a performance by mime artists under the turrets of the Bel-vedere Castle.

The woods were still scented with the white-star flowers of woodland aster on the last day of September, and the full, liquid song from a robin bounced off the trunks and boughs. I wanted to tell the robin to forget his spring song and concentrate on conserving energy for the long winter. But song from robins is not unusual at this time of year. In cer-tain bird species, the glands affecting singing behavior are stimulated in fall and for a few weeks these birds recall the pregnancy and hope and promise of spring, when much about them is dying.

· *October* ·

A kettle of hawks, high in the sky, so high that at times they are mere dots. An impossibly blue sky laced with cirrus clouds, which take the sharpness out of the sun, so it is possible to gaze skyward without blinking and rubbing the eyes. Two ospreys, a broad-winged hawk, and seven or eight sharp-shinned hawks in big circles—lazy, supreme, nothing to touch them.

I had entered the park with an expectation that today would be different, a day not better than most but better than them all. Even at 8 A.M. I knew the temperature on the first day of October would go to eighty degrees, but without humidity or stickiness. My pace had quickened on hearing a blue jay somewhere on a tall apartment block on Lexington Avenue. I had chased a winter wren through the Gill, a waterway forming a series of rapids in the Ramble, and then had come upon a small group of birders studying a fruiting evodia tree in an open glade, which had been good for birds during the fall. "You've just missed an osprey going over, minutes ago," they said and my face registered disappointment. "Damn that wren," I thought and lapsed into the birders' equivalent of self-pity. But the day, with mist clearing earlier, promised more hawks, and I went to the Bow Bridge for a clear view of the sky. Then I saw the ospreys, majestic. I do not think I saw them flap their wings. They were in thermals, conserving energy, letting the rising warm air do the work for them. Then the broad-winged hawk, stubby, chunky-winged in comparison to the ospreys, with three black bands across its tail. Around and above him were the sharp-shinned hawks with elongated tails. I had now tasted the hawk migration, or part of it, and it was not to end all day. At times there were up to twelve hawks in the sky with possibly many more that were higher and out of sight. The broad-winged is classified as a buteo or buzzard hawk and feeds primarily on rodents like rabbits. The crow-sized hawk was heading for a wintering ground somewhere between the Florida Keys and Brazil while the much smaller sharp-shinned would spend the winter months in the southern United States, or possibly as far south as Panama.

During the late afternoon I passed the Upper Lobe and found two young wood ducks dabbling in the weedy mire under the willows. The ducks, scraggy in their juvenile plumage, appeared bewildered and unsure of the journey south. I ventured too close and flushed them out, but I found them a little later sheltering in a dried-up section of the Gill. The waterway at this location was overhung with bushes and the ducks pressed against the shadow of a log. Foolishly, I startled them again, and they smashed through the branches, leaving downy feathers floating behind.

I had thought that the duck migration would come later, and already this misassumption had caused me to miss a rare green-winged teal on the Pond at Fifty-ninth Street. So the day after seeing the wood duck, I toured the lakes and ponds first. At the Belvedere Lake two ducks stood out among about seventy mallards. They were darkish but not black ducks, which were also on the lake at the time. These birds had shovellike bills, which they dipped toward the water, as though the outsized bills were too heavy for their heads.

They were, in fact, ducks called shovelers, two juveniles, lacking the edginess of the wood duck. They appeared at ease among the mallards, which are quite friendly birds, and at one point they ventured close to the bank, unconcerned about me. There was another surprise: an American wigeon in the same crowded area of water. I did not have to raise my binoculars to see the distinctive white crown, which gives the bird its nickname of "baldpate." The bird was a good-looking male, characteristically sitting high in the water. The white crown rested on a line of green feathers covering the eye, and the body was colored a pink-gray.

As I was watching the wigeon a chevron of maybe a hundred Canada geese was flying to the west of the park, somewhere over Columbus Avenue. The geese were in two perfectly straight lines merging at a point. A week later I would see a similar number of cormorants taking the same flight-path. Theirs was a ragged, loose chevron, swaying and bending when individual birds broke the line.

The weather had continued hot and sunny, and on the second day of October I came across the last of the tanagers. This one was a female summer tanager feeding in the evodia tree, a popular birding spot. It was still early morning after I had completed my round of the park and, with time to spare, I decided to look for sparrows, due to arrive in great numbers in the Ramble. Pushing away spiderwebs, which were still hung with silver droplets of dew, I found Chuck from Pennsylvania sleeping in a large hawthorn bush that was still heavy in brown leaf. Chuck was just a rounded shape in a sleeping bag, but I recognized him. I could identify the sack. I began to back off but trod on a dry twig, and he rolled over quickly, as the "snap" ricocheted around the tree trunks of the Ramble.

"What you want?" he shouted, struggling to his feet with the blue quilted bag around his ankles. He held a long knife in his right hand, and he slowly lowered it as his sleepy, semiconscious mind registered it was me.

"You jerk, what you creeping up on me like that for," he said angrily.

"How was I to know you would be here?" I replied, what happened to your home?"

He explained someone had tried to rob him recently, while he was asleep, and he was frightened they might return. "That's what I got the knife for," he said. But I sensed he had always carried it because it fitted neatly in a blue denim waistcoat he always wore.

"Any luck finding a job?" I inquired, trying to make small talk, to be friendly.

"What's it to you?" Chuck said aggressively. "Just go f___ off."

He kicked his foot out of the sleeping bag and there was a clink of glass. A bottle of bourbon had been in the sleeping bag with him.

·   ·   ·

A crowd was being marshaled for the last bird walk of the year on October 3 and, as I approached the boathouse car park, Lambert put two fingers behind his yellow bush hat and started to bob up and down. He was telling me a long-eared owl was in the Ramble. Sarah was doing her bird routine as I hurried to the location Lambert had given, a cherry tree behind the Point Lobe willows. The owl, with his back to me, was about forty feet up, partly obscured by the clusters of leaves. The poor owl, napping after a busy night's hunting, could not have known that in the next few minutes it would be surrounded by the excited people on the walk, most of whom had not seen an owl before. There were shrieks of "Where is it?" The owl swung its head around in almost a full circle without moving its body, to establish what was going on. From his perch he saw a mass of bodies, pushing and shoving, straddling the footpath. Half the people pointed toward him and the others scanned the tree through binoculars. Some of the crowd, being pushed from behind, slipped off the footpath and started to slide down a slope into the lobe. The owl blinked, slowly, as if deliberately assuming a look of amazement. Then it turned its head forward again. The blue jays' cries of hysteria, when they found it, were nothing compared with this. The owl, however, was not to lose it composure. A wise owl stays put and makes the most of a difficult situation, which does not immediately threaten him. I led an old woman down the slope for a better look. A low bush laddered her stockings but, taking me by the arm and stepping carefully, she said: "Young man, I don't care about my tights. I've always wanted to see an owl." It was a good twenty minutes before Lambert and Sarah could persuade the crowd to move on, with most people screaming that they hadn't seen the owl. "But we've got more birds to see and, anyway, we might find another owl in a better position," said Lambert tugging at his hat nervously. He did not let on that the owl is one of the rarer birds of the park, and he hoped no one would realize the promise of another owl was a ruse.

I left the tour and the excitement of the owl to stroll through the park alone, away from the crowd. I found two brown creepers on an oak, a new bird for the fall. And I later heard that the tour had picked up a golden-crowned kinglet. It was another gorgeous day, with a large crowd out in the park. In quiet spots I would find the shy, unobtrusive mourning doves feeding on berries. But my mind was not really on birds today. The park had that bizarre quality again, which produces in me fits of whimsy, of *Homo sapiens Central Park,* a rush-to-the-head of summer before summer finally dies. Children clambered over the Alice in Wonderland statue at East Seventy-fifth Street and, at the park's bowling greens to the south, a croquet game was in progress. Above the white-clad players and hoops and mallets sat an umpire, tennis-style, in an umpire's chair. He was also giving a running commentary through loud-speakers; every now and again there would be a "clud" as mallet hit ball. Did I see one player using a flamingo as a mallet? Had the Mad Hatter joined Lambert and Sarah's bird walk in the Ramble? I could have believed so.

I found a golden-crowned kinglet myself next day when the temperature hit eighty degrees again, and mosquitoes rose like smoke over the corners of the boating lake, where the rocks were coated bottle-green with algae. It was another good day for birds. A black-throated green warbler hopped through the Turkey oaks near the reservoir and I also saw my last black-and-white warbler. The evodia tree, which attracted so many birds, had turned gold, but the majority of trees held their summer appearance. The occasional sweetgum stood out yellow in the same way that the cherries in flower had held the eye in spring. And a red oak was at its peak of transformation. The oily, glossy leaves were alive in death; rich red, and when they fell to the ground, they retained their moist texture for a few days. From a distance a carpet of red oak leaves looked like a pool of blood on a footpath.

•   •   •

A party-goer in what had been a neatly-pressed dinner jacket, bow tie askew, staggered up the slope leading from the boathouse to the Ramble. The gentle slope was too steep for him. He paused to correct his balance by leaning forward sharply. Then he started off again, large patches of dried mud all over his tuxedo, his shirt hanging out at the back. It was noon and the party-goer was on his way home from the party of the night before. He had slept in the park and was lucky not to have been attacked.

This state of inebriation did not appear to be confined to the party-goer. A robin hung his black head low and spread out his wings on the dust of the footpath. He shook his beak from side to side, flapped his wings slowly and spread them out again. I ventured to within a few feet of the robin, but he was unaware I was standing over him. When I clapped my hands to make him fly, he looked at me for a second and tried to give out his alarm cry but it would not come. Then the robin slowly took off with a heavy heave of the legs and settled in a bush only five feet away from me. The birders say robins and other birds partial to fruit become drunk when the vast quantities of berries they eat in the fall ferment inside them. I have my doubts, though. In Africa, veteran white hunters tell stories of elephants getting drunk on the fruit of the marula tree. I have never met a zoologist with experience in the African bush who can confirm this. Many park rangers will tell the story to tourists but will admit they themselves think it a myth when you question them closely. I thought the story of the robins a myth and still do. But I cannot explain the robin's behavior.

·   ·   ·

Ten days after his death, the body of Conrado Mones was still in the city morgue. Rita Serrano was struggling to raise the money for his burial but there was hope for her. The circumstances of Mones's death had received wide publicity in New York. Money was trickling in to the parks department and *The New York Times.*

·   ·   ·

A thick, soupy mist lay on the reservoir on the seventh day of October. The Indian summer and its humidity was clinging, like the sweat soaking my shirt, as I paced the footpath looking for ducks. But I could not see beyond the ill-defined shape of a cormorant, which fished about forty yards from the bank. What I thought was a bat fluttered closer and I realized it was a large monarch butterfly, migrating south. The crickets were chirping and insects still abounded; yet there was a definite feeling that fall had arrived although the trees remained dark, rounded, full shapes in the mist, showing silhouettes of leaves without revealing their changing color. A Chinese woman bent below a gingko tree to pick up nuts, which were falling from the upper branches. The gingko's fleshy seeds are considered a delicacy by the Chinese and the woman's husband had climbed forty feet to risk life and limb to dislodge some of the fruits. If the couple had known of the tree's history they might have been more gentle with it. The gingko has survived from the age of the dinosaur and, with its fan-shaped leaves, it looks like a prehistoric relic. Its family was prevalent over much of the globe millions of years ago, but it died out as the world underwent climatic changes, continental drift, and mountain upheaval. A member of the family, *Gingko biloba*, survived in a corner of China, however, and Chinese and Japanese Buddhist priests later planted it in temple gardens. A German botanist brought the gingko to the attention of the Western world in 1690, and it was finally imported to Europe in the eighteenth century. It is not just the shape of the leaves that gives the gingko its mystery. The seeds have a peculiar smell, which I liken to someone throwing up.

The weather continued misty and humid for the next few days—a massive storm appeared to be building up. A female kestrel crossed the Great Lawn with something large in her talons—maybe a starling—and the birds fell silent as usual, but this time an eeriness was injected into the air, quiet and still. The trees were heavy with dying leaves, sullen, defying the wind to rock them with its full force. With tension between heavy trees and mist-defined air increasing, something had to snap. Crack. Thunder and lightning stabbed across the sky in the small hours of October 8

giving the city the effect of a multicandled birthday cake
with just one ignited candle. Tall, thin skycrapers standing
black and white, stark.

Again and again came the flash of light and then the
crack, which shook windows already vibrating under the
impact of pelting rain. By first light the park was fresh and
clear and a sweetgum had dumped all its leaves over a
bench in the Ramble. The leaves were a foot deep. A swainson's thrush, decorated with yellow cheeks and yellow eye-
ring, looked tired and shaken after being forced down by the
storm, and a yellow-rumped warbler tripped gingerly
through the evodia tree. That night a cold, blustery northeast wind blew. And next day the mean temperature had
switched from an abnormal high to an abnormal low, eight
degrees below normal. Ten ruddy ducks were on the reservoir along with a lone Canada goose and as I watched them
the cold wind bit my ears. Summer had finally let go, and the
ruddy ducks' heads were tucked into warm back feathers,
the birds bobbing on the choppy water.

·   ·   ·

The body of Conrado Mones was laid to rest in a cemetery
over the Hudson River in New Jersey. Enough money had
been donated to pay for the funeral. Some organizations had
even offered to take care of the arrangements, but these
were finally handled by the Parks Department. Before burial, Mones had a mass at a Roman Catholic church in the
Bronx, close to the funeral home which had finally taken his
body from the city morgue on October 8, the day before the
burial. In death, Conrado Mones had been cared for.

·   ·   ·

The ruddy ducks had moved on within a day but five Canada
geese replaced them on October 11. The sounds of march-

ing bands drifted across the reservoir from Fifth Avenue, where New York's Italian community was celebrating Columbus Day with an annual parade. The Italians—unlike the Irish and the Puerto Ricans for their big days—had sunshine instead of rain; but the gentle southwesterly breeze had a bitter edge to it. A bullfrog, feeling the cold, moved slowly under the surface of the boating lake and a green heron struck. The big, bloated amphibian would not see another spring.

I had seen fall's first hermit thrush on October 5, and seven days later the small thrushes appeared to be the most common birds in the park. There were hundreds of them and, in the Ramble, they outnumbered all the other species by about two to one. I did not know it at the time, but I was walking under a tree where a barn owl was roosting. Lambert telephoned me at work to tell me about the owl: "It's between the rustic bridge over the Gill and the wooden pavilion," he said. "There's a lamppost right under the tree with the number, 7535." I could not get into the park that afternoon and by early next morning the barn owl moved out. Although some of the larger owls pose identification difficulties for a person who is not used to seeing them too often, the barn owl is distinctive because it has a white, heart-shaped face instead of the usual disc pattern around the eyes. The barn owl once nested in hollow trees but when Europeans settled the land and built permanent structures, the owl took to nesting in such buildings as farm barns, church belfries, and even in disused mechanical equipment. Basically, the barn owl stays pretty much in the same location all year, but there is a partial migration in the northern United States; and the owl in the park might have been moving only a few hundred miles to a place where there would be a supply of rodents or small birds to keep him fed through the winter.

After work, I went back to the park in the hope of seeing

the barn owl hunting on silent wings, but I only saw two or three suspicious-looking characters in the Ramble and retreated to the reservoir, scared. Reassured by a constant stream of runners, I looked across the blackening water knowing I was safe from attack from behind. I could make out the shape of a cormorant in the distance, and I wondered how long it would remain because most of the cormorants had long since flown south. I did not have to ponder the question long. The cormorant reared like a bear standing on its hind legs, threw out its neck and lifted into the air, the water pulling at the bird's large body and then letting go. Five days later the lesser scaups would arrive from north central Canada to claim the same patch of water for their six-month winter, while the cormorant flew south to claim a piece of ocean off Florida. The laughing gulls, also heading for Florida, remained on the reservoir a little longer and for a time they overlapped with the ring-billed gulls moving to the coast from inland. In the last weeks of October I saw the laughing gulls sitting with the ring-bills in the furrows made by a tractor on the Great Lawn baseball outfields. The laughing gulls had also discovered the fenced-in areas designated for replanting were safe from marauding dogs. The gulls had lost their black-hooded breeding plumage and merely had a dirty patch where the hood had been. They were not as noisy as they had been in the spring, either, and the park would not ring with their laughter.

The lesser scaups had formed flotillas on the reservoir until March when the last ones had left. And now they were back. They returned on October 17, carried by an overnight northwesterly wind. If only they could communicate with me. I wanted to know what adventures they had traveling to the lakes of Canada, as far as the Arctic Circle, where their neighbors were grizzly bears. The scaups have the feel of winter about them, the males with frosty white sides and ice-blue beaks; the females with a white ring of feathers around their beaks as though they have dipped their faces in snow.

It was a special day, one of the better ones of the fall. As I came across other birders here and there I established that there were two birds which would be new species for me. A bluebird was on the Point and in more or less the same location a red-headed woodpecker was also feeding in a mature black cherry.

The bluebird is a small thrush, the male combining a shimmering blue tail, wings, and back with a soft shade of orange on the chest; the female duller but with the telltale blue in the wings and tail. The bird in question was a juvenile but still had enough blue in its plumage to make it unmistakable. Needless to say, I missed the bird, together with the elegant red-headed woodpecker, and I should have been reconciled to my misfortune, but I wasn't.

Next day the influx of interesting, not so common birds continued and so did my bad luck. A hairy woodpecker was seen in a pin oak near the top of the Point and I missed it by five minutes. This woodpecker is a slightly bigger version than the downy, with a sharper beak. The hairy used to be common in the park but seems to be declining over much of its former range. The decline is attributed to the cutting and clearing of its favorite deciduous woods habitat. The species' decline seems to demonstrate that habitat, even if it is only a fraction of what was there once, has to be preserved over a wide range for a species to survive. Birds do not know boundaries, such as those fencing in a park, and must be free to roam to places where they will be assured of the right feeding and nesting sites. The hairy woodpecker dodged me but two rusty blackbirds did not. They were not new species for the year but it was good to see them back again. The male of this couple had lost his jet-black late-winter plumage for the rusty breeding look which gives the species its name—a dainty bird, carefully walking along dead branches in the Point Lobe to pick at insects.

Dogged by bad luck, I had now given up any hope of seeing 150 of the 259 species recorded in Central Park since its opening. By the second half of October I thought that even 130 birds was an ambitious project. But I reached this total on October 21, with two species in one day. First a hairy woodpecker feeding on the Turkey oaks lining the bridle path. Two hours later came what I would regard as my second best find in the park—a flock of five Eastern bluebirds. A northeasterly wind had held promise, and I knew it would probably be the last good day of the southward migration. This proved to be the case. Interesting species that day included a red-bellied woodpecker and a very late waterthrush; but it was the sight of the bluebirds that I will remember. I had left Lambert late in the morning to keep an appointment in town. Because I was late, I broke into a trot near the elm circle, and a bird I could not identify flew from under my feet. It took a few minutes for the mystery bird to settle and, once I had binoculars trained on it, I recognized it immediately. I ran back to the place where I had left Lambert and asked, nonchalantly, how rare the bluebird was in the park.

It was the first time I had seen Lambert run.

We found four more bluebirds, two more males, a female and a juvenile. Lambert said he remembered seeing a flock of twenty-seven in the park when he was a child. He had never seen so many since and said sadly he would never see that number again. The bluebirds had not only lost ground to the starlings but they had also been forced out of the old-style orchards—one of their favorite habitats—by new methods of cultivation and the application of harmful insecticides.

·   ·   ·

The year's last big Central Park crowd gathered on October 24 for the New York Marathon. In all, two million people were lining the streets of New York City to cheer on fourteen thousand runners on a journey from Staten Island to Central Park. A dachshund, tied to a lamppost, barked madly as Alberto Salazar and Rodolfo Gomez raced by neck-and-neck at the twenty-four mile stage of the twenty-six-mile race. The dog went on to bark at the next thousand runners before his owner called it a day and took him home.

Darkness was falling and the robins had long since reclaimed feeding areas taken over by spectators when the race's last finisher, Redmond Dadone, crept across the finish line at the Tavern on the Green restaurant. Dadone was officially listed 13,746th, finishing nearly five and a half hours after winner Salazar's time of two hours, nine minutes and twenty-nine seconds.

In the final week of October up to one hundred scaups started to use the reservoir; on one day they were joined by three canvasbacks, the first since mid-March. The wind now piled leaves in drifts against the reservoir fence and on the last weekend of the month the color-change peaked. The best view was from the south rim of the reservoir, looking north. The line of trees at the top end merged from reds to yellows, to bronzes, to browns, and even to greens: oils on a landscape artist's pallet, round blotches of color with no clear, definite shape but a form and texture all the same. Rainfall the previous week had flooded the Gill and the cold water preserved the richness of a multicolored film of leaves which covered the series of ponds. A yellow-rumped warbler looked for a moment like a tumbling leaf as it chased one of the last insects. Yellow-rumps were few and far between now.

•   •   •

The opponents of the Parks Department's tree cutting program suffered another defeat in October when the Landmarks Preservation Commission ruled a grove of pin oaks could be removed from the Bethesda Fountain area. The trees had been planted as a memorial to servicemen who died during World War II, but the Parks Department argued the pin oaks' roots were undermining the foundations of the elaborate Bethesda Fountain terrace, a centerpiece of the park's original plan. The anticutting lobby had said the trees were too precious to be destroyed. And color slides of tree stumps were not a strong enough statement to persuade the commission to rule against the cutting.

A thick deciduous forest of hickories and oaks covered the area that is now Central Park, when the Dutch first explored and settled Manhattan in the early 1600's. The basic vegetation remained the same until land for the park started to be acquired in 1856, although taller trees among the forty-two indigenous species had been cut down to make ships' masts, and parts of the future park were used for the grazing of pigs and goats.

The exotic forest would come later with the planting of foreign trees but the Algonquin Indians noticed their woods changing irrevocably soon after the arrival of the first settlers. The aliens brought alien plants—often by accident—and the Indians saw unfamiliar weeds sprouting in the undergrowth. On their trails linking fishing and trapping points to villages, the Indians noticed the leaves of the broad-leaf plantain from Europe, which flourishes in open spaces. The weeds' seeds, as with so many plants, came to America in the straw of packing cases or in mud caked on shoes. The spade-shaped leaves of the plantain, which are a common sight on the park's footpaths to this day, were a symbol to the Indians of what was to come and, with an uncanny prescience, the Algonquins called it "white man's footprint."

·   ·   ·

A craggy policeman, the first police officer I had seen on a routine patrol in the park, asked me what I was looking at. I had been so engrossed in watching a wheeling osprey that I had not seen him approach. The policeman had a pinched nose, which tried to make an impression on a round, ruddy, flat face. Hitching up his trousers, which were sagging under the weight of his gun belt, he moseyed closer, pushing back his cap so he could look into the sky for the osprey. The bird circled the reservoir and on the second sweep the policeman caught sight of it.

"Can I look?" he said pointing to my binoculars and, reluctantly, I let him have them. I wanted to look at the osprey myself.

"You sure dat ain't no bald eagle?" he said.

"No it's an osprey. . . ."

"You shur it ain't a bald eagle? I read all about dem when I was a kid."

"No, I can assure you it's an osprey, which is similar," I said, trying to sound like an expert.

The osprey came around a third time, hovered, and did just what I feared it would do. It plunged into the reservoir, scattering the gulls, and rose with a big, silvery fish.

"Goddamn did you see dat?" said the policeman.

"No, you had my binoculars," I replied, digging my toe into the cinder of the reservoir footpath. I could not recall anyone, not even Lambert, seeing an osprey fish in Central Park.

· *November* ·

An unseasonable heat wave enveloped the park on November 1, and the body of a seventeen-year-old youth lay still and cold in the Ramble. The corpse had been found by a jogger in the early morning and as police recovered two knives and three spent .45-caliber shells near the scene of the crime temperatures rose to the upper seventies. It was like summer again—the last of the warblers, the yellow-rumped, chased insects through the willows at the Upper Lobe, which was still in green leaf in contrast to the rest of the park.

The clues to the killing of the teenager were being pieced together the next day when a decision was made to assign two more detectives to the Central Park precinct, bringing its strength to six detectives and a sergeant. The ten killings of 1982 were more than double those in the previous year and five times those in the year before that.

The heatwave, fueled by southerly winds, persisted for the first week of November. Numbers of lesser scaups were still building up on the reservoir, reaching about one hundred and forty birds by week's end when temperatures would begin to drop again.

On November 4 detectives had charged three youths with the murder of the teenager. A routine check at hospitals had revealed the name of a sixteen-year-old boy who received treatment for a knife wound on the night the youth had been killed. The boy admitted being in the park that evening and, along with the two other accused youths, to having committed several robberies. But the three teen-agers said they knew nothing of a murder.

The willows at the Upper Lobe, which had been the first trees to sprout leaves in the spring, started to turn yellow on November 8, the last time I would see the yellow-rumped warblers. By this time police had identified the dead youth as Luis Christian from a missing persons report; then a check of his friends led to a man being charged with manslaughter and to the charges against the other three youths being dropped. Christian and all the others had been part of the same gang, robbing in Central Park. On the night Christian died two intended victims had pulled guns and fired at the youths. In the melee, Christian was stabbed in the throat by his friend, staggered a few feet and collapsed dead.

·   ·   ·

The smell of rotting leaves—the leaves forming a carpet a foot deep in places—filled the woods; a heavy, gassy, un-pleasant odor. Perhaps the pungent smell drove the hermit thrushes south because I was not to see another of the spe-cies before the second half of November.

All the summer migrants had gone now except the laughing gulls on the reservoir, and these would remain until the first week of December, meeting briefly with the incoming Iceland gulls from northern Canada.

The pattern was now set for the winter and the focus of the birders switched to the reservoir. The steady build-up of waterfowl brought its surprises. A female ring-necked duck arrived on November 7 and next day four shovelers, two of them fine males, were seen preening themselves amid the raft of lesser scaups, which spread along the entire length of the west side of the reservoir.

The ducks were oblivious to the human drama and agony that haunts that top end of the park, where lights do not work and police patrols are less frequent than in the busier southern areas. Early in November a woman jogger was attacked as she ran around the reservoir footpath. It was the latest of twenty-five rapes in the park during the year, and on November 13 flyers were handed out to thousands of women taking part in a four-mile race, advising the runners to take precautions.

The titmice and chicadees were also taking precautions when a red-tailed hawk flew in low circles across the Great Lawn and then took in the Ramble in a second sweep. The small birds headed for cover and remained hidden until the hawk passed. But there was another kind of danger which tens of thousands of years of evolution had not prepared the titmice for—a human trap. Bird feeders had appeared in a hawthorn bush in the Ramble, which had retained its leaf late into the fall, and then a birder had seen a man hiding in the bush. The man had a bird cage with him, full of confused titmice and chickadees, which were flying in panic against the bars. The bird feeder contained a sticky substance buried under the seed and this proved an effective method of catching the birds. The birders, however, ordered the man hiding in the bush to release the titmice and chickadees. Protesting in Spanish, the man finally opened the cage's door and the birds flew to freedom. But then he reached into a bag he had at his side, and the two birders thought he might have a gun. They scrambled to safety.

·　　·　　·

Skandy, the polar bear with a record, was not alone in adversity. Soon a postmenopausal gorilla called Caroline and a mean-tempered and distrustful elephant named Tina would share something in common with him: they would all be without a home. Work had started in November on moving two hundred animals from the Central Park Zoo to other locations, in preparation for a renovation program. But homes had not been found for the trio of imprisoned souls, who had brought so much pleasure over the years to the people on the other side of the fence. Tina, who was twenty-five, had been dominated for fourteen years by her late mate, and the death of a trainer she loved had added to her paranoia and anger. She was considered dangerous and zoos were reluctant to take her. With Skandy it was a simple case of reputation, his label as a man-killer; and the saddest case of all was that of Caroline—her only fault being her age, her inability to bear a recipient zoo valuable offspring.

·   ·   ·

I had stepped up my visits to Billy to every second day from the beginning of November because I knew there would be fewer birds to catch when winter arrived. His coat had been growing thick throughout November and the mini-heat wave in the first few days of November made him testy and irritable. At first he had wanted to play, to bite my hand and to be chased across the rocks, but he soon tired of this. He panted with his mouth wide open, dribbling at the tongue, and then looked at me aggressively if I tried to continue the game. Once he struck out with his front paws but stopped short of unsheathing his claws. When the temperature returned to normal he looked happier and encouraged me to stroke his back by arching his spine and rubbing his body against my legs. But Billy never purred, he was not a purring cat.

The temperature touched freezing point on November 16 and Billy was nowhere to be seen. I walked around the outcrop which was his home, calling, but he did not arrive. The bed of grass and leaves in his lair was cold and damp; he had not slept there all night. Maybe he was still out hunting, but it was late morning. He should have been back.

I strolled to the rear of the police stationhouse, to the place where I had first seen Billy, the location of his first lair. He was not there, either, and I began to feel a sickness in my stomach, an ache which was rising to block my throat and impair my ability to talk or think of anything but Billy's immediate fate. I strolled around the reservoir and passed a policewoman, whose curly red hair was trying to fight its way out of her flat-top cap. I wanted to ask her if she had seen a black and white cat, like the one in the Tom Cat advertisements of yesteryear, but I thought she might think me silly, or put me under surveillance as some kind of park maniac. The policewoman was on a newly instituted patrol of the reservoir footpath to deter rapists and muggers, and she walked with a confident stride that did not hide her femininity under the heavy police-issue coat. But her friendly, all's-well smile, was not enough to persuade me to ask her if she had seen Billy.

Every day I went looking for Billy. I left fish at his lair and it went uneaten, and the ache in my stomach intensified. By the fourth day I had difficulty concentrating on my job. On the sixth day of Billy's absence a male ring-necked duck was reported on the reservoir, and I thought the excitement of seeing this uncommon species in the park might take my mind off Billy. On my way to the reservoir I checked the two locations where I had been leaving scrod and was encouraged to find the fish missing from the Ramble lair. But I was guarded in my optimism. Rats could have finally found the fish, I reasoned, but I left a fresh supply at both locations, all the same.

The duck was magnificent, similar to a tufted duck, only with a ring of white behind his neck. But after watching him my thoughts wandered to Billy. I hurried back to the Ramble. From a hundred yards away, through branches now bare of leaves, I saw Billy on the top of the largest rock in the area. He was watching for me. The rock, a favorite sunbathing spot in summer for gays, is situated behind the Azalea Pond. Billy became excited as I approached. I scrambled up the schist, finding a foothold in grooves worn by glaciers forty thousand years ago, and when I reached the top Billy scaled down the far side of the rock. He was leading me back to his lair, jumping from rock to rock, looking back at me and opening his mouth in a silent mee-ow.

He had already found the fish above his lair and had eaten it. He demanded more. Luckily I had some left in my pack and he fed hurriedly, swallowing large chunks of fish at a time. I stroked his warm back, digging furrows in his fur with my fingers.

I had to do something about Billy, but I did not know what. From the time he first came to my hand I had thought about taking him to my apartment, and turning him into a fifth-floor cat, with a litterbox in the bathroom and meals that came in sealed tinfoil packets, the cat equivalent of the television dinner. That scheme, I decided after much agonizing, would not work out. The land beyond the park, of declawed cats, debarked dogs and desqueezed pet snakes was not for Billy. He would not fit in, and I knew he would make a run for it down the fire escape the moment I opened a window. There had to be another answer; for the time being I hoped he would dodge the cat-catchers and the cars on the circular drive, and if he ate any rat poison, I hoped he would die quickly and not bite at his stomach where the poison bit.

•   •   •

Greater scaups, with bottle-green rounded heads, could now be seen among their smaller cousins on the reservoir, and by

Thanksgiving Day numbers of lesser scaups had increased to about three hundred. Ten canvasbacks were with them but the day belonged to a male bufflehead with three females. The white sides of the drake's body stood out brilliantly in the sun and against the sparkling blue water, as though he were a painted, glazed piece of fragile porcelain and not a warm-blooded, feathered creature molded from nature. A cold front from the north had pushed the buffleheads into the park, and I saw the species for three days running, their arrival coinciding with a build-up of scaups to well over four hundred birds, and the sighting of a tufted duck drake on November 28.

The disused children's paddling pool had a coating of thick, crinkled ice and wrapped up warm to keep out the cold was the teenage girl I had seen so often in the park— the beautiful, graceful girl with flaxen hair. She sat on a swing near the defunct pool and kicked backward to start the momentum of the swing. She pressed hard into the supporting chains and moved forward. When gravity pulled, she bent her legs under the seat to speed her motion. In three or four swinging motions she was rising almost as high as the bar holding the swing. The rushing wind pressed her fawn woolen trousers against her legs as if the material were wet and sticking to her skin. The wind tossed her pale gold hair and she puffed her cheeks in exhilaration. The girl caught sight of a young man running toward her. She stopped pushing into the chains so the swing would slow down, and she could drag her feet in the dirt to stop it.

In sign language the young man asked his girlfriend something like, "Are you having fun?"

With her hands, the deaf-mute girl said she was.

•　　　•　　　•

A red-headed woodpecker had set up base in the park during the fall but I had consistently missed the bird, as with so many species in the latter half of the year. The woodpecker was frequently seen gathering acorns for a winter store in an oak near the statue of a husky near East Sixty-sixth Street. The husky, named "Balto," had been the lead dog of a team that carried diphtheria serum to a stricken hamlet in Alaska in the 1920's, and he now looked in disdain at all the pooches wearing their woolen winter coats. A terrier chased a bird feeding on the ground and when the bird took wing I recorded my 131st species. It was the red-headed woodpecker, a juvenile that had not attained its red-head plumage. The barking dog was a minor worry because blue jays had discovered the woodpecker's winter stock of acorns and were trying to raid it. The woodpecker, only slightly smaller than the jays, succeeded in driving them off.

•　　　•　　　•

I had known Lambert nearly eleven months but still did not know what he did for a living, and I would not find out. I did have one more piece to the jigsaw of his psyche. He was a bachelor. He did not tell me this, but I phoned his home one evening to inquire whether he had seen a tufted duck reported in the park and a woman answered the telephone. She said she was Lambert's mother.

Lambert's mother, I was told later, was in her eighties, born in Germany, and, like mothers everywhere, felt it her maternal duty to nag Lambert about such things as his style of dress and his smoking. Among the rules of her home was one that forbade smoking, so Lambert could be seen some evenings taking a puff on the doorstep of their apartment building.

I only spoke to Lambert's mother on the one occasion. When I asked if Lambert had seen the duck, she sounded puzzled. "I don't know. He doesn't tell me anything," she replied.

· *December* ·

More than a hundred years ago sculptors working on a stone relief at the Bethesda Fountain plaza sent to the market for the plumpest, meatiest birds the messengers could find. Flowers and fruits had to be splendid, too, because they, like the birds, were to be used as models for some of the most interesting and carefully executed sculpture in the park. The intertwining motifs of birds in their viney and leafy environment were finished in time for the plaza's opening in 1873, and it now evokes an age when nature's gifts to man were bountiful and, apparently, inexhaustible. The sculptors made the edible birds fleshier and more rotund than they really were, the fruits were bigger and more juicy, and everyone believed the plunder of the wild could go on forever.

The steps leading to the fountain have fallen into disrepair, like so much of the park. And someone has carefully, deliberately, and recklessly taken a blunt instrument to lop off the heads of all the sculptured birds.

·   ·   ·

The willows in the Upper Lobe had capitulated, their leaves turning yellow and dropping into the boating lake. But a giant willow in the more sheltered Point Lobe retained slender ribbon leaves of lime green. The tree formed an obvious hiding and roosting place for an owl and, peering into its branches during the first few days of December, I imagined for a moment I had been transported back to summer. The temperature was way above normal, and rising, and on December 4 it hit a record high, seventy-two degrees, for the month. Air-conditioning units droned on Fifth Avenue and the hundreds of lesser scaups, building up in number to spend winter on the reservoir, looked uncomfortable in the heat, constantly rolling and immersing their bodies in the cool water. The sky was clear but the humidity took the edge off the sun, low in its winter arc. A horsewoman, a pony tail hanging from her black-velvet riding cap, led a group of little girls in a riding lesson around the bridle path, and they were watched by the lonely man standing under the pin oak near the West Seventies.

Chuck from Pennsylvania was sitting on a big rock which protrudes from the Azalea Pond. It was early but the sun was up over the Point, and Chuck shaved a three-day beard with a rusty, blunt razor he had found in a garbage sack on Fifth Avenue. He was not using soap and the shaven portion of his face was red and sore. I asked him if he had a job interview later that day. He thought I was being facetious. I tried to correct this misunderstanding by offering to buy him a pack of disposable razors, but he saw that as another insult to his self-esteem. "I'm just trying to be friends," I said, joining him on the rock.

He concentrated on shaving, finding difficulty without the use of a mirror, and as I was leaving he said without looking up, "You just be friends with that there cat."

•   •   •

A trench-digger entered the Ramble on the morning of December 7, and its mechanical grunting and groaning and roar, when it released a shovelful of mud, attracted a feline spectator. An inquisitive Billy had left the area around his lair and looked down on the activity at the Gill from a boulder near the Indian Cave.

Billy, who was nervous and would not come to me when I called, was not the only spectator. Groups of birders visited the Gill during the day to ensure that the Parks Department was adhering to its promise not to destroy any trees in a new phase of the park's restoration program, which would see the muddy and silted-up Gill dredged and returned to its original concept as a clear-water stream.

Permission for the dredging had been granted after the Landmarks Commission hearing in June, but this decision had been largely overlooked by the birders because of their preoccupation with the tree-cutting issue. All year divisions within the bird watching community had been evident over the degree of tree cutting that was tolerable and the dredging of the Gill, which would only necessitate trees being cut to allow the trench-digger access, finally divided the birders into what can be termed extremist and moderate camps. Lambert had placed himself on the moderate side, arguing that the benefits of the tree-planting program and the general sprucing up of the park outweighed the detrimental effects of the cutting. Many of the birders were not talking to each other and for a time Lambert found himself ostracized by some of the extremists. But the divisions in the birding community did not detract from bird watching itself, and the sight of any interesting or new species would give the birders a common purpose again, and relegate differences to another place and another time.

•   •   •

Policemen and women had now become a common sight in the park and it occurred to me one day, from the park bench of my meditation, that they had come equipped to fight a war. Under the bulky blue uniforms, or attached to them, were the tools of their trade: service revolver, ammunition, heavy torch, truncheon, handcuffs, and bulletproof vest. I got to thinking that next time the United States was confronted by a conflict anywhere it should forget about the Marines and just send in the New York police. It was such a brilliant idea that Lambert, drawing slowly on an untipped cigarette, said he thought I should write to the President about it. "The President of the United States, that is," he added. "Not the president of the city council."

·   ·   ·

Central Park is probably the most closely watched and monitored 843 acres on earth. The debate among nature lovers about what is good for the park is only one aspect of a larger, ongoing negotiation between all interested parties and the park authorities. The parties range from roller skaters, to model sailboat enthusiasts, to botanists and birders, to cyclists and joggers. They all want to extract the maximum benefit to themselves and somewhere there must be a compromise, although the birders, in the main, maintain that nature has been compromised enough in the park, in the city, in the state, and in the country.

Central Park was undoubtedly designed for people, but if Olmsted and Vaux were alive today they might also view the park as a microcosm of the global environmental crisis. They might agree with the birders who see the park as a symbolic last battleground on which man and his natural environment must settle their differences and reach an accommodation with each other that ensures both of survival.

A great horned owl, popularly called the "cat owl" because of its feline facial features of alert eyes and spiked ears, roosted all day in the willow of the Point Lobe on December 8. The owl is about the size of a domestic cat, the biggest owl to be found in the park, and rarely seen. Two birders triumphantly recorded the bird in the sightings register and, after hearing about it, I rushed to the spot at first light next day. The owl had gone.

Two other park residents about to move on were Skandy the killer polar bear and Caroline the aging gorilla. A truck from the Bronx Zoo arrived and it took eight men to roll the tranquilized Skandy into a traveling cage. The forty-five-year-old Caroline (the oldest female gorilla in captivity), came quietly. Zoo officials feared she was too old to be tranquilized safely; they had placed her traveling cage inside the main cage a few days previously, so that she could climb into it, inspect it and satisfy herself there was nothing to fear.

The two animals would stay at the Bronx Zoo until another home was found for them. But even a temporary home had not been found for Tina, the ill-tempered elephant.

Winter was not due to start officially until December 21, but the weather during the year had already proven it did not adhere strictly to a timetable. Winter was firmly entrenched and the maximum number of lesser scaups usually seen on the reservoir—about six hundred—had been reached as the last of the waterfowl came south. Ice gripped the stems of reeds at the reservoir's edge and a huddle of ring-billed gulls stood closely together on a patch of ice in the middle of the boating lake.

Swirls of snow on December 9, and now a grating and slurring of shovels scraping snow from the sidewalk came from Fifth Avenue, instead of the hum of air-conditioning units. The snowfall thickened in the succeeding day, and suddenly the birds of the park had the winter look of desperation about them as they searched for food where the coating of snow was at its thinnest. As in the previous winter, the titmice and white-throated sparrows became incredibly tame and refused to budge from the reservoir footpath, where a sharp northerly wind, a natural snowplow, blew the snow from the path. I looked for raccoon tracks again, this time around a hillock on the east side of the boating lake, where Lambert had seen a group of blue jays mobbing a raccoon a few months previously. Lambert had told me a raccoon's five long claws gave its print the appearance of a human hand pressed in the snow, very different from the rounded paw print of a dog or cat. I found evidence of the steady, trotting walk of a raccoon on a footpath which climbed up the hillock. The prints led to the base of a mature black cherry where snow had been disturbed from crevices in the tree's bark. There was a hole about ten feet up the tree—a raccoon was probably asleep inside, although I could not see it.

In about two inches of snow I also found the oblong prints of the Eastern cottontail on the Point and could clearly make out the tracks of a bounding gray squirrel, which was escaping from a dog. Later I saw a gray squirrel hunched next to a life-size statue of a mountain lion on a rock overhanging the circular drive. The lion had snow on its bronze shoulders and his friend the squirrel spat and growled at a barking dog. The dog backed away.

The blizzard prompted Bill Edgar, who feeds the birds in winter, to commence his feeding program, and I decided I would keep Billy fed on a daily basis throughout the worst months. The feeder area was changed to a location closer to the boathouse. This was fortunate because Billy's lair was near the previous site, and I did not want him to draw the wrath of birders when he caught the occasional chickadee or titmouse. His daily handout from me would make it unnecessary for him to go hunting for birds, and I hoped that before winter had ended I might find a home for him, somewhere in the suburbs but ideally on a farm where he would be a working, rat-catching independent cat.

·   ·   ·

"Let's be friends," I said to Chuck, the last time I saw him.

"There's been a lot of misunderstanding. You got the wrong idea about me."

Chuck had built himself another home after the snow, and he thought about what I had said for a while. "All right. But I got something to say first. It's you foreigners what got the jobs. This city's full of foreigners."

A fire was burning outside the cardboard home, which was situated again under the hidden rock at the Point. There was food cooking in a battered old pot and it smelled good. The fire was a big one; I threw on a stick and Chuck hauled it off quickly. "There you go again. You gonna make smoke and a ranger will come and give me a hard time. I'm moving out this week," he said. "Got money for the fare to Philly. That's nearer my people, my kin. This place is full of foreigners. You gotta be foreign to get a job."

I said nothing.

"I suppose you want feeding, you've come over here because you want feeding."

I shook my head.

"Well you're wise," he said, smiling now. "It's squirrel."

•   •   •

Ribbons of snow, slushy and transparent at its edges, lingered for a few days until a northwesterly wind brought heavy rain to wash its last traces away. Riding on the winds came interesting, if not rare, birds, and in the third week of December excitement increased in anticipation of the birders' main social engagement of the year, the Central Park Christmas bird count. Countrywide, the National Audubon Society conducts a bird census in winter, and this has come to be associated with the Christmas period (Central Park forming one of the zones in the New York City bird-count area).

The snow was doing the best that it could to squeeze itself from a gray-black sky as about forty birders made their way to the reservoir for the census, on December 19. A fine powder had settled in the cracks in the sidewalk on Fifth Avenue. The snow was not consistent or persistent enough to form a blanket, and the birders were happy. A blizzard would have driven birds out of the park and the object of this exercise was to see and record as many as possible. With military precision the park had been divided into quarters, with the Ramble and the reservoir forming fifth and sixth sectors. The general marshaling his troops this day was Dick Sichel, a long-standing park birder, who had sounded out volunteers for this campaign a month previously.

With so many birders vying and trying to outdo each other with birds spotted and identified and counted, Lambert described the event as "the day of the long knives." But he was there all the same and was in charge of monitoring the reservoir. I had been assigned to a party heading to the southwest corner of the park and envied the teams going to the two northern fronts, the high-risk areas of Harlem Meer, the Loch and the Pool where birders do not usually go. In my party was another rookie, the musician with the New York Philharmonic Orchestra, and we were determined to do well in this our first bird count outing. Our first bird was a tufted titmouse, then ten starlings, then twenty town pigeons, two screaming blue jays, and a titmouse again. It went on like that until the viola player, Dawn, found a red-headed woodpecker, and we realized there might be three of these rare birds in the park. Two territories had already been determined; now we invaded another bird-count sector adjacent to ours to see the other two birds and confirm that we were not counting one bird twice. There were, as we suspected, three birds; their territories bordered on each other. They were juveniles, and someone speculated they were from the same brood, possibly raised in the park.

A flicker gave us another species of woodpecker and within two hours we had run out of space and birds to count. Then someone remembered a vague report of a yellow-breasted chat being seen near the Pond at Fifty-ninth Street in previous days, so we doubled back there, because the location given fell within our sector.

Although the chat had been listed on New York's phone-in rare bird alert, it had escaped the notice of most of the park's regular birders. The alert gives sighting reports of any rare species in the New York area, and I could only recall the tufted duck of the previous winter being Central Park's contribution during the year.

We found the chat hiding under a wall which marks the park's southern boundary. It darted into the thick under-growth that covers a slope leading from the wall to the footpath on the southern edge of the Pond. Chasing the chat, I disturbed a hobo sleeping in a large cardboard box; he leapt up in surprise, blinking and rubbing his eyes. The chat proved elusive, and I had difficulty getting a "handle" on him—focusing on him long enough so that I could study every detail of his yellow and green-brown plumage. Then a man, who had already accosted me to explain he was an internationally renowned architect, buttonholed me again to ask me what was the most beautiful bird to live in Ameri-can cities. "I'd say the blue jay," I said impatiently and the middle-aged man, smiling, said his next project, a one hun-dred-story skyscraper, would incorporate the colors of the jay. I did not ask him what an internationally renowned architect, the Sunday newspaper bundled under his arm and an eagerness to talk to anyone who would listen, was doing roaming Central Park on a bitterly cold Sunday morn-ing when he should have been at home in a penthouse reading *Architectural Digest.* I played along with the man's fantasy, missing a second chance to observe the chat.

Outside the boathouse the snow had stopped falling and,

inside, Dick Sichel sat at a table, making notes on a yellow writing pad. The boathouse was crowded with cyclists and joggers and people who had been out walking, and the birders. The air was stuffy and smoky with the cooking of breakfast now going into hamburgers and greasy french fries.

"Anyone see a flicker?" shouted Dick and two groups, including our own, said yes. This procedure continued until the names of all the birds known to winter in the park were exhausted. "Anything else?" he shouted above orders for hamburgers and coffee, and one of our group mentioned the chat. Immediately the boathouse emptied of birders, who scurryied in the direction of Central Park South and the chat. Dick did not notice the rapid exodus. He was busy totaling the forty-two species seen that day, the second highest ever (forty-four being the record, in 1975). Six species of woodpecker were recorded for the first time and among these was the hairy woodpecker, which the Central Park birders have come to use as a barometer of species that are declining in the park.

It is accepted that the bird count cannot be considered a scientific evaluation of species or of numbers of birds, which may be decreasing, or even increasing in some cases, but the high count brought a sense of optimism to the birders. During 1977, for example, only thirty-five species were recorded, and Dick noted that some birds regarded as regular to the park had possibly been overlooked this year. The American kestrel had not been on the list nor had any species of owl frequently seen in the park: barn, saw-whet and long-eared.

Lambert, the Central Park sage, tugged at his beard as he studied the bird count figures a week later. True, they were encouraging but one important point had to be taken into consideration: more people were taking part in the survey than at any time in the past and, with more people counting, it was difficult to make comparisons with previous years.

•   •   •

A statue called the Falconer had been in storage for as long as park users could remember. The nine-foot-high statue depicted a figure who could have stepped from an Elizabethan play: tunic and skin tight pants, soft leather boots and toes that curled up at the end, and a noble falcon, stylized in an aura of romanticism, larger and fiercer and bolder than any falcon would appear in the wild.

During 1982 the Parks Department decided to rescue the Falconer from the stale dankness of the warehouse and put him where he belonged. That was on a plinth overlooking Olmsted Way in the south of the park. In early December a crane lifted the Falconer into place on his plinth, which had been sand-blasted clean of graffiti. The Falconer and his bird were polished and shining and the blue jays began to bypass this corner of the park, believing the raptor was about to launch into the air and fly wild and free.

I had my own ideas about where the statue should be positioned and that was on the stretch of Fifth Avenue paralleling Central Park, officially called Museum Mile. The city council had other masterpieces in mind when the gently undulating stretch of tar was given this name, in recognition of New York's status as one of the greatest repositories of art in the world. The Metropolitan Museum of Art steals a few acres from the park on the west side of Museum Mile and in the 1,760 yards is also the Solomon R. Guggenheim Museum.

I saw all the galleries and museums in my first few months in New York and found them an anticlimax. I thought they were overshadowed in that location by a bigger and more glorious work of art, born of New York's sweat and ingenuity and not imported from Egypt, India or Greece. The masterpiece is, of course, Central Park; and the fact that silt from its eroding surface clogs drains on the Museum Mile says much for the city's priorities and values.

In 1982 a Central Park renaissance began in earnest to correct some of the devastation of the 1970's when New York was on the verge of bankruptcy. The restoration program would cost $100 million over ten years, over and above the annual running costs, and Central Park administrator Elizabeth Barlow admitted the city would not be in a position to meet this cost. Much of the money would have to come from private or corporate sources, channelled through the park's main fund-raising body, the Central Park Conservancy, if the work was to be completed.

•   •   •

A little black girl with long hair in wiry pigtails sang "Oh Come All Ye Faithful" from a bench in the shadow of the Simon Bolivar statue at Central Park South and the Avenue of the Americas. Five youths selling drugs stood at the top of the flight of steps leading from the park to the street, and I pushed my way past them in pursuit of the yellow-breasted chat again. Five days had gone by since I had seen the bird on the Christmas count, and I was curious to establish whether it was still in the park. I only had to wait ten minutes, nervously eyed by the drug-sellers, who thought I was a cop, before I found the chat. I was standing on the street, looking down on the tangle of bushes, which were laden with berries and home to the man in the cardboard box. A passerby threw bread for the pigeons into the dip and the chat came for this, carrying off chunks of it. I had always believed chats were insect-eaters but the bread and, I suppose, the berries supplemented a winter diet of hibernating bugs. Two wood ducks, a male and female, had been seen on the same day at the Pond, but I could not find them myself. I moved on to the zoo and was in time to see Tina, the bad-tempered elephant, being fed like a condemned prisoner, in a cell of yellow tiles and blue-gray

bars. Four loaves of bread and two basins of mixed veg-
etables were emptied through the bars and Tina, calm
and relaxed, rolled whole lettuces in her trunk and tossed
them into her mouth. She also gathered three carrots at a
time, balancing them in the hairy lip of her trunk, and tossed these after the whole lettuces. A sign in an adjacent,
glassed-in enclosure said the resident Indian python
had been moved to the Bronx Zoo; there was still no
home for Tina and a home would not be found by the
year's end.

·   ·   ·

I scouted a farm in Orange County, New York State, for a
home for Billy. The farm was owned by a business acquaint-
ance but there were two cats there already, fierce and
fighting, and I knew Billy would want to be master of his
own environment. I was confident Billy could dominate the
cats finally, but there was a chance he might run away in the
transition to his new surroundings. I did not want to take
that chance.

I asked Lambert if he knew of anyone who might want
a cat. He came up with the name of a shopowner on Lexington Avenue, who had a daughter living in Southampton on
Long Island. I went to see the shopowner and, by coinci-
dence, his daughter was in New York on a shopping trip. She
had a big property, away from main roads, and she also had
a mouse problem in some outbuildings. But she was reluctant to take Billy at first, until we both agreed on a trial
period. This was acceptable, and I noted a softening of atti-
tude when I took the drugstore owner's daughter to see Billy
one afternoon in December.

Billy, of no fixed address in Central Park, was to become
a Long Island fat cat.

•   •   •

Christmas Day in Central Park. Joggers jogged in new track-suits, which were still creased from being wrapped as Christmas parcels, and little boys rode new bicycles that had not yet been scarred and scratched by the curb. The patch of worn ground under the pin oak where the lonely man had stood all year was deserted; the pin oak appeared exposed and forlorn without its companion. I was happy for the lonely man because he obviously had somewhere to go for Christmas, friends and kin other than his pin oak. But there were people in the park without friends, no one to share Christmas gifts with and with no gifts to take back to the shop next day to be exchanged for something a little bit smaller, or something a different color, or something else. A woman of about forty, who looked fifty in a pale, lined face, stood on a rock in the boating lake where black-crowned night herons had stood in the early morning in spring. She was wearing a fake fur coat although the temperature, at sixty-four degrees, equaled a record high set in 1889. Slowly she bent and scooped a handful of dirty water with cupped hands and then wiped her coat with a brushing motion. She started on her hair, as scraggy and spiky as the fake hair of her long fake coat.

A red-bellied woodpecker stole my attention as it flashed black-and-white-and-red through the trees. I followed the woodpecker north, through the Ramble, through Wild-flower Meadow, beyond that, to Muggers' Wood, without looking back at the woman washing her hair.

The lonely man was back under his pin oak the day after Christmas, presents were being exchanged in shops removing their Christmas decorations, and a male wood duck slept on a branch ten feet above a batch of roosting mallards on the Fifty-ninth Street Pond. But I was not paying much attention to the goings on in the park. I was worried about

Billy again. I had not seen him for four days, and now I searched the Ramble, calling his name, moving in widening circles until I had covered the whole of the bottom end of the park and the Boston scrod was beginning to smell in my pack.

I had a sleepless night, after dreaming Billy was four blocks away in the park, dying in a storm drain on the circular road. By morning I had convinced myself I was being unduly sentimental about this animal. It was only a cat after all, its immediate fate out of my hands, so why should I worry and care? I headed north through the park, defying muggers, and I told myself the reason for this excursion, with the whole day to myself, was to find the remains of fortifications from the war of 1812—relics I had overlooked during the year. That is what I told myself, but when I reached the stone-walled Blockhouse, the most important historical site in the park, I did not bother to squeeze through the narrow door into the pebbled courtyard inside. Instead, my eyes followed the winding circular drive from where it left an old Manhattan coach route at McGowan's Pass. I was looking for Billy. In the first curl, the snaking road swept around the hilly site of Fort Fish, crossed the lower end of the Loch and then came around the Blockhouse in what was virtually a complete circle. Below me, a machine for smoothing ice worked in tight circles on the man-made ice of the Loula D. Lasker Pool as I left the Blockhouse to walk back along the west side circular drive. Under a beech near 101st Street I counted five juncos, the first I had seen in weeks, and there, five feet away from the road, I saw the body of Billy.

•   •   •

Billy's coat is rich and shiny. I cannot see any obvious sign of injury and I will never know how he died. I can only surmise he was hit by a car and do not question why his body is lying away from the road, in a quiet, sheltered place under the beeches. I don't want to think of him crawling there to die or of someone picking him up on the road and placing him on a soft bed of crinkled leaves. I find myself a stick and dig as deep as I can, through layers of compacted leaves, the leaves darkening into a gray, pungent tar as I dig a foot down, and I hit the roots of the beech and can dig no farther. Carefully, I lift Billy and place him in the hole, tucking his black and white face, like the one in the Tom Cat advertisements of yesteryear, under his left paw so it hides his eyes. I kick dirt on top of him, trampling it down and walk away briskly. After about ten paces I realize I am running, and it stays that way until I enter the city beyond the reservoir and I have had enough of the park.

·   ·   ·

There is nothing like the smell of Boston scrod, not spoiled yet but about to get that way if it is carried around in a pack any longer, for attracting the attention of a raccoon. The day after finding Billy dead I had been about to empty my refrigerator of a pound of scrod when I remembered the raccoon living in the black cherry near the boathouse. Late that afternoon I went to the spot and laid out the scrod a little way from the base of the tree. The squirrels avoided it, but a crow showed an interest before I chased him off. Strangely, the weather was humid for this time of the year—with another record high—and I could smell the scrod from fifteen feet away. The raccoon, however, was not stirring. I waited half an hour, and when I saw the staff of the boathouse cafeteria pass nearby I began to get nervous. The cafeteria had closed, darkness was falling, and the park looked dangerous. I was about to leave when I saw a movement somewhere deep in the hole in the cherry tree. I could see hairs just behind the rim of the hole and then two eyes, glistening and catching the light from a street lamp on the circular drive. And then a full, round head and a masked face with an inquisitive, twitching nose. The raccoon gripped the rounded edge of the hole with its five-clawed paws and hauled its head up, but seeing me it dropped inside again. After a minute or so the raccoon, nose still twitching, leaned out of the hole to see where the smell was coming from, but it would not leave the safety of its hiding place while I was there. I even tried backing off about twenty yards, but the raccoon was too nervous to climb down the tree. It was nearly dark now and I left the park, and the raccoon to the scrod.

Within two weeks of its discovery, the drug-sellers at Central Park South become experts on the yellow-breasted chat, its feeding habits and its location at any given time. The peddlers, who usually numbered five thin youths, sought out people carrying binoculars and asked politely whether they were looking for the bird.

"It was on the left side of the path leading to the Pond," one of the youths, a gangly black kid of about nineteen, told me on December 31. He reminded me, politely, that he had "coke and the golden smoke" just in case the sight of the chat did not give me a sufficient high.

I had been wary of the drug-sellers at first, thinking they might be muggers, but I now regarded them merely as businessmen, and I felt secure with them around, because I knew they would not allow a mugger onto their lucrative patch.

The chat looked set to stay for winter and so did the pair of wood ducks on the Pond. Like the chat, the drake and his mate had also taken to eating bread thrown for the park's avian residents.

The wood ducks' acceptance of handouts of bread filled me with a bleakness, a despair, a realization that what mankind offered with one hand was taken back with the other. The wood duck and chat were not to know that the very habitat they need for survival—at both ends of their migration range—was being snatched from them. Warblers, orioles, tanagers, flycatchers, and thrushes were arriving in the Caribbean and in Central and South America to find tropical forest turned to farmland. Ducks were also losing wetlands. An article on migration in *Smithsonian* magazine late in the year had said tropical rain forest from Mexico to Amazonia was being cleared at the rate of 100,000 to 250,000 acres annually, possibly affecting the long-term survival of many species of migrants. There could be a time when the birds I had seen during the year no longer came through the park. The wood duck and other species of waterfowl that do not leave the United States have more serious problems. In this country alone, half the 215 million acres of wetlands that once existed have disappeared, and I read of a recent study indicating that nearly half a million acres were now being lost annually through land being drained for agricultural uses and housing development.

The light faded at 4:30 P.M. and I had just enough time to see one of the red-headed woodpeckers, the last bird I would seek out in 1982. Since the Christmas count twelve days previously, the birds had acquired much of the red plumage on their heads, and they would be looking beautiful by mid-January. The red feathers would form the shape of a roman gladiator's helmet and, as I watched one of the birds along the Mall, I thought they should have been named helmeted woodpeckers. A helmet might also come in handy when it was time to open their store of acorns in late winter, and defend the stock against an army of hungry blue jays.

The red-headed woodpecker had been my one hundred thirty-first bird when I first saw the species in November and that would remain my total at year's end.

· · ·

At the stroke of midnight the sky over Central Park exploded in a thousand fireballs of white, yellow, green, and red. The blast startled a flock of ruddy ducks into flight at the reservoir and a carriage horse, carrying revelers on a trip around the circular drive, bolted out of control. The horse and carriage careered into the tightly packed vanguard of nearly three thousand runners in an annual midnight marathon. Some of the runners were wearing tuxedos and top hats, some were dressed in animal costumes and historic fancy dress. There was panic and screams as the athletes fell under the flaying hooves of the horse and the high, spoked wheels of the carriage. The horse, unharmed, was brought to a halt a few hundred yards along the road and ambulances were called for the thirteen people who lay injured.

The race continued, as relentlessly as the coming of 1983.

The fireworks gave stroboscopic illumination to the skeletal branches of the park, to the apartment cliffs of Fifth Avenue, and to Central Park South and West for five minutes. Then there was an explosion of gold stars, packed together, taking the shape of a giant oak in thick leaf, smoke trails forming the contours of its bark and trunk. A doorman stuck his head from the entrance canopy of a Fifth Avenue apartment block. He had witnessed the fireworks more times than he wanted to remember; when he saw the golden oak in the black sky he waited for a last spray to rise above the fireball tree and a last ear-shattering explosion, which cracked and thundered across the east and west side of the city.

And he said: "That's it."

· · ·

Lambert found some white-footed mice, not in Central Park

but farther afield, on Staten Island, and he drew a crayon and ink picture of the indigenous rodents.

"When you get past the traffic, buildings, and turmoil the real world remains," he wrote in his first letter of the New Year, "there is not a great deal left but enough to let us retain our optimism."

Checklist of the Birds Seen by Donald Knowler in Central Park during 1982

Double-crested Cormorant
Great Blue Heron
Green Heron
Black-crowned Night Heron
Canada Goose
Mallard
Black Duck
Gadwall
Blue-winged Teal
American Wigeon
Northern Shoveler
Wood Duck
Ring-necked Duck
Canvasback
Greater Scaup
Lesser Scaup
Tufted Duck
Bufflehead
Ruddy Duck
Sharp-shinned Hawk
Red-tailed Hawk
Broad-winged Hawk
Osprey
American Kestrel
Solitary Sandpiper
Spotted Sandpiper
American Woodcock
Common Snipe
Least Sandpiper
Iceland Gull
Great Black-backed Gull
Herring Gull
Ring-billed Gull
Laughing Gull
Rock Dove (Feral Pigeon)
Mourning Dove

Black-billed Cuckoo
Long-eared Owl
Chimney Swift
Ruby-throated Hummingbird
Belted Kingfisher
Common Flicker
Red-bellied Woodpecker
Red-headed Woodpecker
Yellow-bellied Sapsucker
Hairy Woodpecker
Downy Woodpecker
Eastern Kingbird
Great-crested Flycatcher
Eastern Phoebe
Barn Swallow
Blue Jay
American Crow
Fish Crow
Black-capped Chickadee
Tufted Titmouse
White-breasted Nuthatch
Red-breasted Nuthatch
Brown Creeper
House Wren
Winter Wren
Northern Mockingbird
Gray Catbird
Brown Thrasher
American Robin
Wood Thrush
Hermit Thrush
Swainson's Thrush
Veery
Eastern Bluebird
Blue-gray Gnatcatcher
Golden-crowned Kinglet

Ruby-crowned Kinglet
Cedar Waxwing
European Starling
Solitary Vireo
Red-eyed Vireo
Philadelphia Vireo
Black-and-white Warbler
Worm-eating Warbler
Blue-winged Warbler
Tennessee Warbler
Nashville Warbler
Northern Parula Warbler
Yellow Warbler
Magnolia Warbler
Cape May Warbler
Black-throated Blue Warbler
Yellow-rumped Warbler
Black-throated Green Warbler
Blackburnian Warbler
Chestnut-sided Warbler
Bay-breasted Warbler
Blackpoll Warbler
Prairie Warbler
Palm Warbler
Ovenbird
Northern Waterthrush
Louisiana Waterthrush
Kentucky Warbler
Common Yellowthroat
Yellow-breasted Chat

Hooded Warbler
Wilson's Warbler
Canada Warbler
American Redstart
House Sparrow
Red-winged Blackbird
Northern Oriole
Rusty Blackbird
Common Grackle
Brown-headed Cowbird
Scarlet Tanager
Summer Tanager
Northern Cardinal
Rose-breasted Grosbeak
Indigo Bunting
Purple Finch
House Finch
Common Redpoll
American Goldfinch
Rufous-sided Towhee
Dark-eyed Junco
Chipping Sparrow
Field Sparrow
White-crowned Sparrow
White-throated Sparrow
Fox Sparrow
Lincoln's Sparrow
Swamp Sparrow
Song Sparrow

The Falconer of Central Park
has been produced by Izora Cohl, the editor.

The design was executed by Abby Goldstein.

It was typeset in 11/13 Caledonia with
Bembo display.

The Maple-Vail Book Manufacturing Group printed
this edition on 60 lb. Warren's
Old Style Wove paper.

The map used for the endpapers was furnished
through the courtesy of the New York Public Library
Map Room and is printed on
80 lb. Simpson filare.